To Laura
I love you —
Glad we are
after so long.
Blessings
Barb

Practicing MEDICINE
"I Don't Think That Word Means What You Think It Means"

BY BARBARA SHEFF TOCCI

RoseDog Books
PITTSBURGH, PENNSYLVANIA 15222

RoseDog Books
701 Smithfield Street
Pittsburgh, PA 15222
Visit our website at www.rosedogbookstore.com

ISBN: 978-1-4809-9850-6
eISBN: 978-1-4809-9872-8

DEDICATION

To my dear husband Michael, whose selfless love and care has seen me so tenderly to the other side of this season. He (I think) loves me more than ever, now that my "right hook" has been disarmed by the stroke. To my six sons, who have allowed me to call them whatever name came to mind first (or second, or third...), who pitched in to keep the farm running and the house from total chaos. You boys were great big brothers to Myles. Thank-you for taking over while I "vacationed" for 6+ months. To Helen Sheff, my mother, and head cheerleader. When I said, "I want my mommy" you came. Thanks for coming to my aid, and for just listening. Patricia, my sister, and Don, my brother, thanks for always being there. I knew I could count on you. For all those who cooked meals, babysat Myles, helped my rehab effort, and prayed unceasingly for me. Thank-you! To Michael's family who, along with my mom, purchased the hyperbaric chamber to aid my recovery. What a huge blessing that was. To my mother-in-law, Ruth Tocci, and my dear friends, Andrea Garrett and Jane Weber, for all your painstaking efforts in editing. My "brain fades," (missing words) grammatical and spelling blunders were no match for you ladies. You make me look good.

Above all, to my God: thank-you Papa. Only You could make this "pile of ashes" into something beautiful. You, who made my heart, healed it. Thank-you for keeping Your end of our "deals." You are Faithful. You are my Rock, and the Lover of my soul! I'm so glad that the order for my new body has already been placed.

CONTENTS

PROLOGUE

When Barbara woke me for the second time in the early hours of December 18, 2007 with the words, "Michael, I think I am stroking...", I immediately perceived a cataclysmic shift in the axis our little world. As it was, it had been slowly losing its grip for several months. Soon, it would be far more than that. As it became clearer over the next several days, weeks, months and years, not only had there been a complete change in the direction our little world was spinning, but there had been a radical alteration in the orbit in which it was traveling. While sitting in the emergency room, waiting and waiting for someone to do something other than ask Barbara (who was precipitously losing function right before their eyes) stupid administrative questions, I remember hearing a little voice saying, "You have now entered the Twilight Zone..."

In revisiting her story, I can attest that Barbara has been thoroughly honest. I was there at every gruesome turn in the road. I mean, who else could be? (Not that there weren't times I wished I could have found someone else). We have six inches of medical records to back it all up. And as much as I'd like to wish them away, the stark memories of these times have lost none of their definition. When I let my guard down, they wander in. For this reason, (I will openly admit) that in reading the early drafts of her book, for which she had asked my assistance in editing, I sincerely hoped that Barbara would be content with simply getting things off her chest and onto paper, and be done with it. But this was not to be the case. After a couple of half-hearted attempts, I begged off. I just couldn't take it.

In the family in which I was raised, as in perhaps most, we have a tradition of burying matters such as this, fast and deep. I have heard attempts made to justify this as a matter of self-preservation, with a strain of fatalism. "It happened, get over it." (There are bumper stickers out there that state the sentiment in somewhat cruder terms). Such a matter had occurred much earlier on in our marriage, going on three decades ago, when we lost our infant daughter, Caitlin Avrit. I can only view that tragedy as an entirely preventable accident, and despite the doctors', and everyone else's, opinions to the contrary, my heart knows what it knows. "Bury it, and move on..." is the only other counsel available in this tyrannical vernacular. But it is, in its very essence, the vernacular of moral cowardice, which I am very glad is in no way shared by my wife. Barbara is the most singularly courageous person I have ever met. Because of her undaunted courage, she can afford to be brutally honest.

It takes courage to revisit the times and places of tragedy. It takes more courage to revisit these events with the knowledge that heartbreak, sorrow and bitterness are close-lurking dangers. These are unavoidable, but they are not invincible. With the ever-present help of her God and Father, Barbara has passed through this valley of the shadow of death, and come out the other side, full of life and grace. This book is a record of that journey.

Now, here I must attest to the thousands of hours of meticulous research, writing, rewriting that Barbara has invested over the past three years in producing this book. Added to this are the hundreds of hours of review and editing invested by three of the finest grammarians I know: my mother, Ruth Tocci, our long-time friend, Andrea Garrett, and our sister-in-arms, Jane Weber. Their invaluable assistance has refined this work without compromising the essence of its expression of Barbara's forthright character, and the sense of humor and perspective that have been preserved by her undaunted courage.

However, as some things being slow to change, I am personally glad to see an end of it all.

Pax vobiscum.

1. The Hospital Room Window

We were homeward bound after five days in Virginia; I was staring mindlessly out in the darkening landscape. As we sped back to New Hampshire, we passed a large hospital along the highway and I was drawn by the light shining in one of the patients' rooms. Suddenly, fear – lurking in memories that lay smoldering in my soul – seized me. My heart started racing as the memories of many a dark hour spent in the clutches of a very prominent teaching hospital in central Virginia came flooding back like a wave. It startled me, causing me to sit upright in my seat and do battle against those demons of fear and horror once again. It was then and there I knew I had to write this, for healing sake.

It was as though I was no more than a laboratory rat, as numerous doctors "plied their trade" on my poor sick and suffering body. An undefined illness had the best of physicians scratching their heads. Their response had been to grasp at straws, through the application of a multitude of powerful drugs, guessing at the reason why they were using them. Blindly aiming at a target but never hitting the bullseye. At times their "trade" cost me dearly, even to point of losing parts of my body, initiating events that were going to forever alter my life.

2. The Old Me

Ah yes, my body. I was one of those rare people who loved my body. For years this corporal vessel had served me well – even magnificently – I would say. Athletically inclined from an early age, I always was pushing the envelope and it had risen to every challenge. And there were many!

In my younger days, every summer in my town of Hamburg, New York, there were held athletic games called Junior Olympics. My favorite competition was 100-yard dash. I would sprint down the track in worn-out sneakers leaving my rivals in the dust, just as my mother had done years before when she was young, an example of the "fruit not falling far from the tree." Then it was around the frozen rink in winter, only this time on figure skates. Everyone else had racing skates. I told myself figure skates would allow me to win with finesse. Sure, truth be told, we didn't have the money for racing skates. It mattered not; I was undefeated on the rink. During the long winters in that suburb of Buffalo, no one grabbed MY hat and got away with it. I played football with the neighborhood boys and always was first round pick because I was fearless. I threw passes like one of guys and tackled like one, too. In high school I was voted Most Athletic, and I suspect if there had been a category "Most Obnoxious," I would have walked away with that too. I went to college to study Animal Science, where I wrestled cows, pigs and horses with equal tenacity.

From my youth, my body had been put to the test. Scarlet fever, Measles, dragged by a horse, kicked by a few, hit by a baseball thrown 90 miles per hour, while playing catch – a game of catch played in the rain, and the ball was wet. It glanced off my glove, hitting me just below my eye, breaking a bone in my face. It seemed I spent half my high school years on crutches. I had all the usual childhood diseases plus a few more just for good measure. It was life at 100 mile per hour, even on the turns. My mother was a registered nurse and it was a good thing. Her training was constantly put to good use. When I was 11, I fell into a coma for seven days under the grip of Spinal Meningitis. I recovered fully, much to the surprise of my doctors who were sure I would suffer residual effects of some disability or permanent damage. God was merciful; we had just lost my father to a massive heart attack the year before. This was just what my mother needed after suffering such a loss. That being my history as child, as I began to have children, I innately trusted doctors. They had saved my "bacon" often enough, I can say, and even my life. Our family physician came to the house late one evening when I had severe symptoms from meningitis. It was Dr. Mattimore's accurate, swift diagnosis and treatment of meningitis that kept my Mom from having to bury a daughter a year after burying her husband. These doctors lived in my hometown; I went to school with their children. Physicians had always been my friends and allies, until one event that changed my outlook, not so much about doctors – that would come later – but about the practice of medicine in general.

We were living in New Hampshire after my husband graduated law school. Having been married about seven years, we had four children at the time. I was 32 years old, "healthy as an ox" as my husband loved to say, but I contracted whooping cough. I remember the day I met the "donor" of that nasty germ. I had gone to my chiropractor for an adjustment and he had a patient who was "whooping" her head off. Within six to seven days I had what appeared to be a simple cold and after three weeks was in a full-blown case of whooping cough. It is not called the "100 day cough" for nothing, "24/7 100-day" cough is more accurate. My husband, who was practicing law out of our garage turned office, was spelling me when he could, in the care of our children. I would catch catnaps sitting in a chair in my bedroom during the day. I was getting zero sleep at night because I was having coughing spasms every time I would try to lie down. I would have them even while sitting in a chair at night. It always seemed to escalate in the evening.

Full disclosure: I am a Christian and I talk to God and He talks to me. Well, I was continually discussing my situation with Him. Truth be told, it was more along the lines of complaining. He repeatedly told me I would do well to go to the little health food store in town. I felt the tug to talk to the owner about my health issues or just "demo" a coughing fit for him. The doctors had been no help to me. Every couple of days they would give me oxygen treatments, pat me on the head, and say "Honey, get some rest." They could do nothing that would stop the wracking cough. I was exhausted. The antibiotics they gave me were just as useless.

About this health food store. My feeling was that this long-haired, leather coat clad man, known as Jay Constant, would not be much help either. "God, look at his hair." Yup, I am ashamed to say, that was me 25 years ago. I'm surprised now thinking back on my prejudices, that God did not remind me that His Son did not have a crew cut. But I digress. I relented and went to see this hairy fellow who reminded me of a biker, with his leather coat and long locks. Desperation had set in. I had been to the store once a few weeks prior just to check it out, see what they offered. The store's owner, Jay, was in. I went to the counter to talk to him and it didn't take him long to see the awful shape I was in. Maybe the bags under my eyes or my coughing fit when the warm air hit my lungs tipped him off. I asked if he had anything that would tackle this persistent cough. He told me that he had "just the thing". How many times had I heard that before….? Wellllll, did I eat a bowl full of crow. I swallowed my bias of men with long hair along with the crow. In 24 hours, the herbal tincture combination that he GAVE to me worked. Yes, I said gave to me, saying, "If it works, then you can pay me. If it doesn't, you owe me nothing." This medicinal tincture brought my coughing under control almost immediately. In two days, I was sleeping through the night. Sweeeeet. I went back to pay him the next week and to "pick his brain." I had to know what this was and how it had worked so well. Interestingly, the major ingredient was mullein, a large, ugly "weed" that grew at our home around our deck. I had pulled it out because it was so invasive, not to mention ugly. Mullein leaves tinctured in alcohol, (gin, vodka) are excellent for breaking up the mucus in the lungs and are very soothing to the membranes. Growing right outside my window was my answer. Jay Constant was a Naturopathic Doctor, and I picked Jay's brain for the next 15+ years until a tragic accident took his life in 2009. I had grown to care deeply for this wise, generous man. He had mentored me, holding nothing back in the process. Now, I pick his wife Doris's brain, but after nearly 20+ years it's more like collaboration. We remain close to this day.

3. Art of Natural Healing

Thus began my journey of wild crafting and cultivating specialized herbs for medicinal applications. My family was my captive audience or sometimes lovingly referred to as my "guinea pigs." I read every book I could get on the topic of natural healing. By the time my boys were old enough to wander the fields, we had moved to Virginia. We lived on 300 wild acres and they were always bringing home herbs, flowers, and medicinal plants they recognized from photos in the books I was reading. I'd show them the plants that were native to our region and sooner or later they would find them. It was not long before I was sharing what I knew and my concoctions with my friends and helping their families heal with what God had provided in nature. The only time we went to the doctor back then was for broken bones. Even our livestock enjoyed (using that word figuratively) my new found skill of herbal healing.

For example, we were out riding one summer day and my horse, who had a history of being afraid of his shadow, bolted when a huge truck passed us on the road. He hit some barbed wire that was lying in the grass on the side of road. The wire tore his leg wide open from his knee to his pastern, just above the hoof. I was able to close a huge, gaping wound on my horse's leg that the veterinarian said would take a month, at least to close. It was healed in two weeks using Comfrey compresses. In fact, Comfrey heals the skin so fast you have to watch for pockets of flesh below the skin. The skin, which heals easily compared to flesh/muscle beneath that can take longer and can fill with fluids. Whether or not my horse "enjoyed" the treatments is anyone's guess. Before long, the word got out and people would call to consult with me about the best herbs to use for an ailment. I held tincture parties, teaching the art of making medicinal tinctures. Herbs, the leaves or the roots, were steeped in 80-100 proof alcohol for two to three months then administered by drops under the tongue. When I went to the liquor store to get what I needed for ten ladies making tinctures, asking for eight bottles of vodka or gin, I was given the, "Well, I never!!" look. Eventually, they asked me why I needed such large quantities of alcohol? Now, when they see me come in the store, they just ask, "How many?" I would also teach the ladies how to make ear oil out of fresh ground garlic and the small yellow Mullein flowers, both of which have proven anti-microbial properties. What would you rather have when you have an earache – antibiotics, which wipe out all the good bacteria in your gut or garlic/Mullein flower steeped in olive oil? Fire in your gut, or warm and soft oil in your ear?

One of the most satisfying, successful applications of herbal healing was the disappearance of a tumor in a Yellow Labrador's head. A neighbor we knew owned a wonderful male Lab. One day he came by our home to break the news that his dog had a tumor, and the veterinarian had given him three to six months to live. We were all devastated, as the boys loved the dog and would play with him for hours. Mr. P. knew that I had experience using herbs medicinally. So he asked me if I had anything that would help his beloved dog.

I told him I would research the best, most effective herbs to use. I ordered some tinctures from my best source for tinctures. In four days I handed them to him. I gave him instructions how to apply the tincture, topically and internally. His dog's next appointment with the veterinarian was in six weeks. I was apprehensive about trying to restore his dog's health with just herbs. I tried to explain that it was a long shot, an experiment at best. We should look at this as, "nothing ventured, nothing gained."

The report was that the tumor had stopped growing after six weeks of using the herbs. Three months later, the veterinarian told him, "Whatever you are doing, keep it up. The tumor is shrinking." It took ten months, but it was no longer visible on any scan of the dog's head. There was great rejoicing in the "hood" that day!!

Coupled with the study of herbs, I began to study the human body, the how and what makes it tick. I began to research diseases and their signatures on the body. I learned what medicinal herbs to apply to a malady, and how to prepare those herbs.

While still in New Hampshire, I began working with a doctor who did home births. We had our children at home, except for one. This was my husband's idea, at first. Before we were married, he had lived in Bridgewater, Massachusetts, in a home built in 1653 by John Alden's oldest son. The house had a birthing room. That's all it took to plant the idea firmly in my husband's head. "I am going do the same thing with my children!" I'm so glad he led us in that direction.

I wanted to help other women experience the joy of birth unhindered by stifling hospital protocols and drugs. This doctor, Peter Hope, was a kind, gentle man, like a grandfather that everyone loved. He and I would come to a birth and if it was not progressing, he would catch some "shut eye" as I stayed alert with the mom. I learned so much from those experiences. When we moved to Virginia, I worked with a couple of midwives assisting in deliveries. For excessive bleeding we would use Shepherd's Purse that I had tinctured from the wild-growing plants along the fence line on the farm. Comfrey, for healing the tears that come with a big-headed baby, or one that was in hurry to meet his family. Several of my sons had problems with persistent bloody noses, and Shepherd's Purse worked immediately to stop the flow of blood. Between what I learned about medicinal herbs and proper nutrition, we never had to go to the doctor.

One day, I got call from a close friend whose son had a tick bite that had begun to form a ring around it, accompanied with a low-grade fever. These are telltale symptoms of Lyme Disease caused by a parasite that infects ticks. The usual course of action would have been a round of antibiotics. This mom didn't want to take that route. Cajeput oil is a powerful oil from the Melalueca tree, the "big brother" to Tea Tree oil. It was my standard treatment when my boys would come home with ticks. One or two drops and the tick would pull its head out and die, or it would die and then I could extricate it. It also served in preventing infection. I had never put it to the test for a case of Lyme in this early stage, although it was purported to stop Lyme

Disease in its tracks especially when it's used at the onset. I suggested she apply this oil four to five times a day and in three days the ring was gone, as was the fever. The same oil would stop an ear infection, strep throat, and congestion from colds when rubbed on the chest, with olive oil.

After nearly 20 years of using natural remedies on my family and others with great success, I thought I was prepared for anything. Coupled with prayer, there had been nothing in the raising of my own six sons and caring for myself and my husband which I was not able to apply herbal medicines to successfully. That was, nothing yet.

I preface my story with this bit of history to give you a picture of who I was prior to getting sick, and my M. O. (modus operandi) was dealing with illnesses. I thought I was extremely self-sufficient, but not reckless. So, when my prayers and standard herbal and holistic treatments were not working as I had hoped, I didn't hesitate to consult a medical doctor. I did not understand how locked-in the medical profession was to allopathic medicine or how closed minded they would be to my working WITH them to regain my once-vibrant health. I'd been out of touch with that realm in many ways, for a long time. I did meet one physician that prescribed a battery of alternative holistic therapies. I engaged his services late in the game, after much damage had been done by drugs, tests, colonoscopies and so forth. He was "rowing against the tide." Even this fine physician was stumped by this illness's signature on my body. Here's how the drama began.

4. The Beginning of the End

I was going at life full throttle, home schooling my youngest two sons, and working very part time in Real Estate. We had a huge, bounteous garden. A dear friend, Nanette Glaser, had a herd of Alpine dairy goats. They were beautiful, and boy did they produce a lot of milk. Nannette sold me my first purebred goats. Before long I was running a herd of 25 dairy goats, producing and selling goat cheese and goats milk soap. I had 35 or so chickens and various other livestock. Our youngest two sons were a very integral part of the operation of the farm. From collecting eggs to pulling weeds, even my six-year-old had his part to play. I had started teaching kickboxing and was part of a co-ed soccer team with my husband. I enjoyed my

The Tocci family and the author's mother, Helen Sheff.

motorcycle or horseback riding on the weekends. I was basically having a great time. Life was good and FULL.

A friend asked me to take care of her "Newfies." Newfoundland dogs, for those who are not familiar with the breed, are huge, beautiful, hairy dogs, like big teddy bears. She had seven of them at the time in her kennel. She was planning to visit her brother, who lived out-of-state for two weeks. My son, Andrew, and I took turns feeding them twice a day. Things were going very smoothly. One of the duties was to take a small shovel and clean the dog run. One of dogs had very odd-looking droppings, wrapped in mucus, streaked with tinges of blood. The strange "poop" showed up every day, and I became concerned that one of the dogs had a parasite infestation. I talked with a veterinarian about what I had observed and he suggested that they needed to have a stool specimen checked. He told me that his son, who worked with him in his clinic, had contracted parasites and had a dickens of a time getting rid of it. This was from a dog they had boarded. He recommended that I should be careful. When I'd come home from my friend's house, I was sometimes pretty dirty, between the drool, hair, and dirt from the pen. I'd always shower AFTER I fed them. I won't keep you in suspense, sure enough in three weeks or so, I was having odd loose bowel movements several times every day, and I started to lose weight. I thought it was some kind of intestinal bug, which would soon end. Now, I'm sure this next little tidbit falls into the "too much information" category, (a place I often find myself) but here goes. My bowel movements started to resemble the dog's poop that I had called the vet about. I immediately started my regime for parasites, eating carefully, mostly bland foods, so as to not irritate my intestines any more. I was using the "big guns" in fighting this attack. It seemed to be helping, things returning to normal. Then, it would start up again. Hindsight is a wonderful, and sometimes irritating thing.

Using herbs is different from antibiotics; they don't hang around in the body a long time. When administered under the tongue they enter the blood stream in seconds, which is good. They pass out of the body, taking their effects with them, in a few hours, which is not good. I realize, looking back, that they needed to be present in my system all the time. This was war, and if you're not pushing the enemy out

ALL the time it gets and keeps a foothold. The life cycles of the parasites were coming into play continually. Every two or three weeks, new larvae were hatching, taking the place of any that I had wiped out. I knew about the life cycles. I cannot explain this lapse in judgment. I was going to pay dearly for this mistake.

There are several points of entry for parasites to gain a foothold in the human body. The obvious cavities are the mouth and nose, but they can even enter through the skin and eyes, endangering not only the digestive track, but every organ in the body, including the brain. They can even at times be fatal, if left untreated. Not wanting to lose any more weight, and watching my vitality slip further and further away, I decided to consult a gastrointestinal specialist. That's when I made my second mistake, and it was what started the cascade of events that ultimately led to my stroke.

5. Enter...Ciprofloxacin

Now, I'm not going to "bleed" all over in my telling of this tale. I seek no revenge, and I am not looking for a row of scalps for my mantle, despite my Indian lineage. Rather, I'm going lay out facts as they happened, and as I remember them. What happened to me, my husband refers to as a medical "perfect storm." Having raised six very active boys, I never had experienced something like this. We had weathered a lot of medical issues. This happened to me, who had taken the "bull by the horns" to wrestle any infirmity to the ground until it said "Uncle!" Up to this point, like my record on track and on the ice, I was undefeated.

Going to a gastroenterologist, I was expecting a discussion, a meeting of the minds, questions and answers. Boy was I wrong. I was weary, weak, and vulnerable, and this could not be disguised. The appointment lasted about 20 minutes. Dr. L. wanted to do a colonoscopy right away. So much for discussion. A colonoscopy seemed inappropriate to me on many levels. That, "Let's just take a peek," was just what I didn't want to hear. Where am I, at the gynecologist? I tried to explain this was a parasite and that my symptoms were identical to the Newfoundlands I had cared for. It was becoming very clear that, I was talking to a wall. He had patients waiting, like cattle in a chute, ushered in, ushered out, chop, chop. He had no time to ponder what I was saying, and no time for silly little "anecdotes" from a silly, dumb blond. He made the pronouncement that we would try Cipro to combat the problem. To me, this sounded like using a bazooka to kill a fly. In my condition, with no other options being presented, I reluctantly agreed. I knew Cipro was a big gun, used for

Third World country infections, and for ANTHRAX! That was then. It is not the case now. They are using it almost like aspirin, and people are suffering because of that. *

Cipro was going to kill all bacteria in my gut, the good and the bad. I was a little skeptical about how Cipro would deal with a parasite. By this point, however, I was so blinded by my misery. I had lost 20 pounds, and had only ten to spare at the onset. Desperation clouded my judgment. I could have said "no," but coupled with his observations and remarks, my confidence in my prognosis was being undermined. I began to wonder whether it WAS something other than a parasite. Or maybe this regimen WOULD kill the parasite that I was sure was the culprit. I took the prescription he handed me and left. Michael, my husband, knew of my aversion to drugs and we talked about just waiting to see …if…. No, we would get the Cipro, three days' worth, and hope for the best. My thinking was what could just three days do to me? As I look back at this cave in, I'm still wondering, "Who was that woman?"

When the first round did nothing, Dr. L., true to form, prescribed a second, higher dosage, five days' worth. By the end of day three, in the second round, I was not only having violent diarrhea but I was bleeding, and was in pain. Needless to say, I never finished the Cipro. Pain is going be a reoccurring theme in every part of this saga. From here on, pain and I were inseparable. If I had known what the future held….. well, it is just as well that I didn't. I went into battle mode, for I was in a battle for the restoration of my health, and, it felt like to me, for my very life. Little did I know that it was not that far from the truth.

I was continually seeking God for answers, as was my husband. A few good friends were praying also. It appeared to me that I was on my own. I felt like I was drowning and there was no hand reaching in my direction. A whole lot of soul searching was going on inside. Was I missing the message or lesson? Was I just so distracted with my misery to hear God's voice? Was everyone else who was praying deaf, also?

Losing weight week after week and the pain in my gut every time I went to the bathroom was terrible. I began to research this new foe, not knowing what it was in name, but in symptoms it was clear. I felt very threatened and I knew that this was something that was above my pay grade. I contacted my good friend and Naturopath, Dr. Jay Constant, my "long-haired biker friend" who ran the health food store.

Jay's advice was based on his experience helping others, and his then extensive research into what he suspected to be in my case, ulcerated colitis. I felt that his counsel was something to take seriously. What he advised was Slippery Elm powder and several healing herbs, also herbs for combating the parasites. Within a week, there was some definite relief, and the bleeding abated, but it didn't stop completely. The pain greatly diminished, but it was not healing all the symptoms. The "trots" continued. I didn't learn until much later that Slippery Elm is, on the surface, very healing to the mucosa in the gut, but is a mucilaginous polysaccharides complex, (complex sugars) which can feed the bad bacteria. The damage that the Cipro did to my colon was something he'd not seen or experienced with anyone. Not only was my gut very damaged, but it was also devoid of beneficial bacteria, despite taking probiotics. My weight kept dropping, and Michael and I agreed to a colonoscopy. As I write this, I shake my head, knowing what I know NOW about colonoscopies. "Let's just take a peek" had won the day, and I gave in to it, and also to the rigors of preparation for the event. I think this was another decision that accelerated my demise.

I was instructed to drink a strange solution that was to clear my intestines. They warned me to stay close to the bathroom. By this point I pretty much had dibs on the bathroom at my house. "Urgency" was already part of my day; this was "explosive urgency." I read the prep directions on a web site and it said "colonoscopy prep can get boring." I'm sorry, but this was obviously written by a dim wit or someone who never did prep before. My life was VERY exciting. I was getting more exercise than I did teaching kickboxing and I was anything but bored. "Wear loose clothing, and arrange for some privacy as you are going to experience high volume, **high velocity** diarrhea," the web site instructed. "Velocity" is a word that never should be associated with a trip to the bathroom. Now, I ask you, does this sound boring? After all the "volume and velocity," when the time came for the colonoscopy, the doctor said I had ulceration in the area of my colon that they could see, but there was much they could not see. Three days of prep had failed to do the job as intended. So not only had I done all that prep for nothing, but I had succeeded in decimating any residual good gut flora. I stepped up my probiotic intake, but it didn't help. The trots just kept getting worse.

Prednisone was the next drug they wanted me to take. Having some knowledge of the side effects from a close friend who was on it for a year, I declined. My conclusion is that the Cipro caused the damage to my colon. Upon reading other reviews of this drug, there were a myriad of side effects including "**ulcerated colon with bleeding**." More drugs, more unintended side effects. I'll pass on the Prednisone. Back to the drawing board. It was my goal to research what had worked for others who were dealing with similar issues. In hindsight, the Prednisone was the drug that MAY have helped, at least in quelling the inflammation that was now rampant in my body. When I read that one of the side effects can be gastrointestinal upset and ulceration, I was not willing to risk more insult to my colon.

*(.http://www.navytimes.com/apps/pbcs.dll/article?AID=2013311010 018)

6. My Very Own Stent

Rapid weight loss causes a release of extra bile, which is made in the liver then stored in the gallbladder. Stones can form when the bile, which is there to digest the fats, begins to form tiny "pebbles" that can get lodged in the bile duct. Never had I felt such direct communication from my gallbladder before. It was screaming "SOS" at me now!! The pain was intense and constant. Again appealing to God for direction and or relief, I got neither. My usual response would have been an herbal one, fasting on apple cider for 24-36 hours, and then olive oil, which is a very effective way of dissolving, and/or dislodging a gallstone. Not this time. My bowel movements were slick enough. So I waited, just about three days and it passed. I was writhing in pain day and night until it passed. I used castor oil packs on the gallbladder and that gave a little relief. The second time a stone was lodged, I went to a doctor. He REALLY wanted to remove my gallbladder. I knew it was coming. So I educated myself on the pros and cons of a life without a gallbladder. "No, definitely not, I'm very attached to my gallbladder," I told my doctor. After the third attack, not able to convince me to part with it, they decided on placing a temporary stent in my bile duct to keep another stone from lodging. After the stent was in place, everything quieted down.

It was around that time I found an elemental diet that I began to use as my complete diet; it was my only substance at every meal. There were three flavors: chocolate, strawberry and vanilla. The only flavor my body would tolerate was vanilla. The bleeding stopped and my weight stabilized. I never gained weight while on it, no matter how much I drank. It was tolerable to drink, but not great. Now

THIS was boring. For someone who had to cook meals every day for my family, and who loved to cook and eat, not being able to partake was hard.

My life stabilized somewhat. My trips to the bathroom became predictable, less painful and things seemed to be healing. I read all I could get my hands on on the subject of colitis. The intestines and the colon calmed down a bit, but there was constant systemic inflammation. I set to work getting in my daily routine, as many anti-inflammatory supplements that I could. Bosweilla, Turmeric, Omega 3s, glucosamine-chondroitin, B Vitamins, Folic acid, Vitamin D. This list varied, but these were some of the core weapons in my arsenal. I did the elemental diet for months on end. It was very easy to digest, but the good bacteria never could get a foothold, despite taking probiotics. My gut was desperate for the bacteria that keep the flora in balance. Ever since the two mega doses of Cipro, that balance eluded me. Not to mention the ulceration in my colon that was still present. Every time I tried to eat anything solid, it would cause bleeding.

Though I knew God had not left me, He was silent in all this. He was letting things run their course, allowing me to be put to the test. He knew the beginning and the end.

That summer went fairly well. I used the elemental diet, swam as much I could in our pool, let life slow down to a mere crawl. My blood work still showed the inflammation markers in my body were very high. Then I did it. I fell. Like the ballerina that I am not, it wasn't pretty. On a day in the early Fall, there was a freezing rain that caused ice on our back steps leading out to the barn. I was heading out to milk the goats and I slipped on the stairs. I tried to catch myself, but couldn't. I landed hard on my back. I asked my son to milk the goats and I went to my room to gather myself and assess the damage. I had a huge bruise on my back where the spleen is. Now, I had been having pain in that area. So I'm not really sure what came first, but I had somehow formed a clot in my spleen. An ultra-sound of the area showed this, later at the hospital. If I didn't have pain prior to the fall, I would say the clot was from the fall. "The chicken or the egg." What came first is a mystery to this day.

When I had a scan taken of my injured spleen, about 30 percent had infracted, meaning it had died from the loss of blood circulation due to the clot. To this day, I still shake my head in disbelief; they wanted to take my spleen out!! I'm seeing a pattern here: first the gallbladder and now my spleen. What next? If I didn't know better I'd think they were selling used, "New to you" body parts, "Seconds," "Slightly used." You get the picture. Well, we explained to the Doctor, that even 70 percent of a spleen is better than no spleen, in our, granted, uneducated opinion. We'll take a chance that 70 percent will do the job. I suffered through two infractions from the clotting. Each time I was in terrible, blinding pain. The 70 percent of my spleen was working overtime. Despite the pain, I was not going to let anyone talk me into removing it. The cumulative effect of my misery, and the many encounters with physicians who refused to consider anything I had to say as valid, started to take its toll. My new-found inability to trust ANYTHING that anyone wearing a white coat said, no matter how sincere they seemed.

There was much discussion, by all my doctors, about the clotting going on in my body. The blood work said that the fibrinogen count was very high. Inflammation can cause this phenomenon. That was their best guess as to why it was happening. My question was, what's causing the inflammation? I'm quite sure the colitis was playing a part, but that, I believe, was only one piece of the puzzle. Blood that clots excessively can lead to a heart attack or stroke. Fibrinogen is the protein found in blood plasma that allows clotting, I had too much of a good thing. So my doctor's solution was another drug. This time, it was one that is used to kill rodents.

7. Enter...Coumiden

Warfarin, or Coumiden as it is often referred to, was a drug I was familiar with. My mother had to take it at one time, and my next-door neighbor had been on it for years. I knew it had to be monitored very carefully. So they told me to come and have my blood checked every two weeks. Knowing my history with drugs, a little goes a long way, so I asked to have it checked once a week. They didn't think I would need that. I was ready for this fight. He finally did agree to every week for a month, after that, we would go to every two weeks. I consented to that plan. I was started on a fairly low dose. Everything was going well for about two months. I had my blood monitored every two weeks. They were constantly adjusting the dosage. It seemed my body was very fickle. I began to be concerned. I asked them to change the monitoring to once a week. This was refused. During the following week, I woke to huge bruises all over my thighs and my stomach. I called my Doctor immediately. He suggested I come in the next day. My blood was running very thin in my body. Time to adjust it again. Coumadin stays in the body for two to three days, and I was taking it everyday. Maybe it was the cumulative effect in my blood stream that was causing problems.

Around the third month, I began to have bruising again and this time it was worse, larger, bleed outs. It looked like I had been in a fight and lost. We discussed yet another drug, in the form of a shot. It cost about $75.00- $90.00 a day, depending on where I bought it. The least expensive of that particular medication was from Canada. We tried this type of medication for while without any real problems. The biggest drawbacks were the cost, and Michael was giving me the shots. He was already pushed way outside his "comfort zone." My doctor thought we should try the Coumadin one more time, since the cost of the shots was such a financial burden. The timing of this it is a bit blurry, but I think I was on Coumadin for about a month when one morning I woke up with a huge bruise on my hip and buttock, and few on my arms behind my biceps. There were multiple wounds on my legs, my breast, my stomach and my back. I had the appearance of a burn victim. The wounds were dark and getting darker all the time. The one on my hip and buttock was the worst, it was nearly completely black by the next day and it was very painful! I called my doctor and told him what happened. This was now the entrance into a bad dream that I seemed unable to wake from. How is it possible to break myself out of this chaos? When is this going to end?

After the doctor examined me, he said he believed, they would absorb back into my skin and diminish over time. I break out in a cold sweat revisiting this time in my life. It seemed, in fact, that I HAD relinquished care of my body to the "experts" and it was not going well, to say the least. Who was this person? Why did I allow this? How do I get off this train, and can I do anything to fix it? God, where are you?

8. No to Natto

A month or so earlier, prior to this, I started to go to an MD who practiced integrative medicine. Doctor A. was familiar with alternatives to drugs, such as herbs and supplements. I had been researching nattokinase, a natural blood-thinner.

Natto has been used as a folk remedy, primarily for diseases of the heart and circulatory system, for hundreds of years. Nattokinase, the chemical in natto that is probably responsible for its effects, was discovered by a University of Chicago researcher, Dr. Hiroyuki Sumi. Nattokinase decreases the ability of blood to clot. In fact there's evidence that it dissolves clots. Natto thins the blood and might protect against conditions caused by blood clots such as stroke, heart attack, etc. Dr. A. was aware of its properties but had a limited range of personal experience with it. His wife and partner in the practice was also working on my diet, as I had begun to go off the elemental diet. This dear couple (she was a dietician and very well-versed in complementary and alternative therapies) tried, with every bit of knowledge and wisdom about the body, to help me. We reached some level of stability, but by the time I employed them, the damage to my body's systems was very deep. The inflammation was systemic, and every inch of my poor, tired body was rebelling. I was desperately looking for an alternative to rat poison. I began to use the nattokinase as I tapered off the Coumidan under the direction of Dr. A. Doctor M., who knew nothing about alternative therapies, asked me to stop taking it. I ended up taking it for about two weeks. I was torn between two voices. Now, with the Coumiden having this effect on me again, I wished I had just gone ahead and weaned myself off it four to five weeks earlier as I had planned. I was hoping to take back some control that I had WILLINGLY given up. I blame myself first for every thing that had transpired. I took the drugs, but I didn't have to. Yes, I was in a weak and vulnerable state, so I have a reason, but in my heart of hearts, to me, that was not a good enough excuse. Looking back at this I truly felt like a pawn, being played in some cosmic drama.

9. Pain in the Rear

I had my son, Myles, my seventh child, at age 43. No, my being pregnant at that age was not a surprise. It was a SHOCK! Michael almost fell over when he learned the news that I was once again pregnant. "How did that happen?" I thought it was kind of late to give him the ol' "birds and the bees" talk. All this time, I thought he knew. In his defense, the physician that delivered our sixth child by Cesarean section, told us that the chances of another pregnancy were very slim. Oops.

Myles was about six years old when this was in full-blown crisis. I can't even remember how I coped with a child his age, better yet, HOW HE COPED!! I vaguely remember reading books to him from my reclining chair that I bought to sleep in. It was too painful to lie down. This young child had to watch my suffering, not being able to help except in small ways. (He is now 13 and is so compassionate, sensitive to other people's needs. That's one of the ways God made lemonade from the "lemons" that were being dealt to us.) I was barely holding the house together, cooking meals, doing laundry. I had bleed-outs all over my body. One was nine inches long and seven inches wide on my right buttocks, and in the spirit of fairness, I turned the other cheek and had a smaller one on that side too. The doctors we were working with (using the word "with" figuratively) didn't believe it was the Coumadin causing the bleed-outs. They felt it was an inflammatory response to something else going on in my body. A biopsy of one of the wounds proved to them that I was suffering from a condition called vasculitis. But, why? To me, that was the million-dollar question. My take on that diagnosis in retrospect is, "You'd have increased inflammation in your veins if you had rat poison running through them for months." But I have no initials after my name. They did not see the medication as ONE of the causes. I had all different kinds of doctors stacked sky-high, all shaking their heads with wonderment at my body and what it was doing. I would end up being "a case study" for some med students. I am going to be famous…. or infamous, rather. Let me state here and now that I don't think they were purposefully causing injury. Some of my doctors were very caring and kind, but thoughtful? There didn't seem to be one thoughtful doctor among them (the exception being Doctor A.). No one, it seemed to me, after I left the office after an appointment, seemed to give my case another thought. "Whew, she's gone." Next?" seemed more likely. I'd happily be proven wrong.

To me, the best doctors don't ask you to check your brain at the door, or what you know about your body. I <u>knew</u> my body. Right at the onset, they denied this fact, and I turned into their worst "doctor nightmare." In most of their minds, I believe they felt I knew only enough to be dangerous. But what THEY knew, proved to be just as "dangerous." When physicians are part of the system they're not free to think outside the box. They have to follow protocols to cover their backsides to keep from being sued. Most follow cookie-cutter protocols, leaving little to no room for a situation like mine. My body was following no rules, coloring way outside the lines. No set formula was working. Drugs throw a whole other set of variables into the mix, side effects creating their own problems, multiplying the drama. It appears, that the "practice of medicine", has been reduced to peddling of drugs.

I recently read a book entitled, *When Doctors Don't Listen: How to Avoid Misdiagnoses and Unnecessary Tests*, by Leana Wen and Joshua Kosowsky. This book exposes, as the writers call it, the "cookbook" approach to diagnosing illness. With an actual algorithm formula to decide what tests, what risks, and then what treatment is called for. In their words, the patient goes through an "assembly line." What's wrong with THAT picture? It validated the impression I got at the gastroenterologist, Dr L., "just cattle in a chute" experience.

The wounds all over my body were very painful, and a solid night's sleep was elusive. I would go through every day trying to find a comfortable position and a place to rest. Then after two weeks, something terrifying started happening to the large wound or hematoma, as they called it. It began to peel off my body. Like a slab of raw dead meat it was ripping away and there was not a thing I could do about it. It was one inch thick in places, filled with old blood, tearing from my body, nearly to the bone. Damn, there goes my career modeling lingerie.

We called my physician to explain what was happening, but he did not want to see it. Instead, he sent us to a plastic surgeon. This felt like a classic "buddy pass." The plastic surgeon took one look, and I mean one look, gasped audibly, and told us to go to the hospital to have my right "cheek" de-brided. "De-what?"

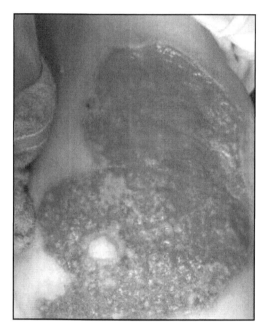

I liken the process of debriding to power washing a deck. The technicians gave me a shot of a fantastic, mind-altering drug that did not really knock me out, but just put in a state that I really didn't care what they did to me. "Man, I could find uses for this stuff," I remember thinking. (Anyone who has had any dealing with goats understands why this thought crossed my mind.) I was placed naked as a Jay Bird onto a metal table that had a gutter on the edges. They proceeded to "power wash" the wound off my body. I remember the technicians making small talk about what they had done that weekend. I remember thinking, "Are you washing a car, boys? (Most men do not multitask.) Pay attention to what you are doing!" When I got a hold of my wits again, I was being wheeled to my hospital room. The wounds behind my biceps, stomach, thighs etc. they left to resolve over time. Those were not peeling off, as they were not as deep.

Michael was in the room waiting for my return. He asked how it went. I said, "See for yourself." The nurse lifted the sheet to show the results, and his face went white with shock. The "hole" was huge. He was not prepared for what was left of my hip and buttocks. It was bright red, raw flesh, like nothing we had ever seen before. "Well, they finally got a piece of me." It had been a long wait and unfortunately for them, it was unusable. I fought the fight for my gallbladder and my spleen, but there was no alternative with my "right cheek."

"Mrs. Tocci," my doctor said, "We don't believe the Coumadin has caused this event." Here is just <u>part</u>, of what I discovered about Coumadin.

*"Although rare, Warfarin (Coumadin) can also cause skin tissue death (necrosis) and gangrene requiring amputation. This complication most often happens three to eight days after you start taking Warfarin. If you notice any sores, changes in skin color or temperature, or severe pain on your skin, notify your doctor immediately."**

If that doesn't convince you that the Coumadin caused my skin to bleed out and fall off, then this next "possible" side effect might do the job.

"Severe bleeding, black stool or bleeding from the rectum, skin conditions such as hives, a rash or itching, swelling of the face, throat, mouth, legs, feet or hands, <u>bruising that comes about without an injury you remember.</u>

Each web site gave me basically the same litany of dangers that could present themselves while taking Coumadin.* One particular site was very informative. **"Necrosis of skin and other tissues."** and <u>***Vasculitis!***</u> **
Where have I heard that word before? Vaculitis is also listed as one of the side effects of Cipro. But I could never convince the men and women in the white coats that Coumadin was what most likely caused a nine by seven inch by one inch thick piece of my derriere to fall off.

*(http://www.mayoclinic.org/diseases-conditions/deep-vein-thrombosis/in-depth/warfarin-side-effects/art-20047592)
**http://www.healthcentral.com/druglibrary/408/coumadin-side_effects_drug_interactions.html

10. Does Anyone Read the Charts?

Once in my room, an aide or a nurse proceeded to put compression wraps on my legs. SCDs, sequential compression devices, as they are called, are "leggings" that go the whole length of your legs, mid-thigh to ankles. SCDs fill with air to compress, then release the legs, to keep your blood moving, to prevent clotting. She placed them on each leg, turned the machine on and left the room. Michael and I were discussing when we thought they would let me go home. My feet started to hurt and in a few minutes, the pain was excruciating. The color of my feet was changing. We called for the nurse, no response. Michael went to the door, looking down the hall, no one was around. I was writhing in pain, so he shut the compression machine off and we removed the wraps. Enter stage left, the second shift nurse. Michael had gone to the cafeteria to get some lunch and I was alone when the new nurse came in to look at my chart. This, incidentally, said that I had been diagnosed with vasculitis. What happened next is hard to fathom. She started to put the wraps on me again. I told her very plainly that I didn't think that was a good idea, and that last time they were on it was painful. She refused to listen and assured me SHE would make it so it didn't hurt. Like a fool, I let her. That I let her, this was the "hard to fathom part."

The nurse left my room, and in a matter of minutes my feet and ankles were screaming at me again, and my feet were going dark. I called for the nurse to come back. I am sure that my yelling was akin to the psych ward at the state hospital, but didn't care! I was unable to reach the machine myself. I was trapped in the grip of this device that was cutting off the circulation in my feet. My husband burst in the room, surmising immediately what happened, and ran to shut off the device. My feet, especially my left foot, was black, all the way to the instep. Michael went get to the physician who was on the floor. He returned with a doctor who, upon reading my charts, showed his obvious disgust. He proceeded to place an 8 x 10 sheet of paper on my bed that read "NO SCDs" But the damage was done. He was aghast at what they had done to my feet. He then proceeded to find the nurse who disregarded my request to not have the SCDs placed again on my legs. When someone, in this case ME, has vasculitis, SCDs are a big fat medical "no-no". (After the dust settled, we went through all my records and discovered the company that makes the SCD units did not have any warning labels whatsoever for conditions that make their use inadvisable.) They waved every "magic wand" over my foot they could think of but, alas, my foot was not coming back to normal. My husband suggested Nitroglycerin, which helped some. That evening, when Michael went home, I lay in my hospital bed, fighting back the tears and the hopelessness I felt about my situation. Looking at myself, wounds everywhere, pain wracking my body, I was a modern day Job. When is this going end?

Having gone to the hospital for de-briding my wound, I went home two days later from the hospital with blackened, dying toes. They drew lines on my feet to show how the black from the blood was receding and the flesh was returning to normal. By the end of the month, my foot was much better except for two toes and a patch on the ball of my foot. I was in pain 24/7. As the nerves in my toes died, they screamed their departure. I was going lose those toes and they were not going go out quietly.

Just recently, on a hunch, I reviewed a letter I had received in return from an inquiry I had made into the use of SCDs on me. A. K., an RN, was at the time of her letter, the clinical coordinator in out-patient care at a major hospital in Alabama. I was curious to know if the use of SCDs could have been the cause of the clots that wreaked havoc in my brain. (We have, since that letter, discovered it was most likely the Amicar drug I was given. Clots that form in the legs can cause pulmonary embolism, or heart attacks, not stroke.) I just made my inquiry in general terms, just to find out what the protocol would be using SCDs on a person with vasculitis. This was her response:

"*As you know, Vasculitis is an inflammation of the blood vessels. The arteries, veins and capillaries may be affected. There are many conditions that may cause or contribute to vasculitis: such as **medicine**, issues with the immune system, diabetes, or infection. I don't know you and neither do I know anything about your physical condition. Therefore, this information may not address your needs. The best person to explain this to you would be your health care provider.*" She went on to say: "*SCDs act as a constricting device that is designed to improve circulation and prevent clot formation originating in the lower extremities. A person diagnosed with vasculitis has blood vessels that are inflamed, fragile and are not functioning properly. The surrounding tissues are sometimes inflamed also. By using SCDs on a patient with this condition; one may traumatize the tissues causing ulcers or cause more damage to fragile blood vessels.*"

The biopsy I had done two weeks prior said that I had vasculitis. A.K. mentioned that one of the causes of vasculitis "could be MEDICINE." What medicine I had been given up to this point? Cipro, a big gun, for big bad germs, two rounds. And Coumadin, a blood thinner approved for humans (used to kill rats/mice), four to five months.

11. House of Pain

I went home to recover from the hospital stay that had been for the sole purpose of debridement, and now, compounded by the erroneous use of the SCDs . I was unable to walk due to the condition of my left foot. With the help of my husband, I would get around to the bathroom and to our living room to lounge on the couch or on a reclining chair in our bedroom. Sitting was tricky with the crater on my hip and buttocks.

You might wonder how I knew the exact dimensions of said hole. Well, I had good friend who came to my assistance. A veteran in the nursing field, she had seen just about everything! An RN, PTA (Physical Therapist Assistant) with 15 years of wound-care experience, with nine years of skilled nursing and long term care experience, Sandy Milazzo was a fearless and compassionate help to me. Her sense of humor was always like a drink of water in the desert. She had a positive attitude all the time when she came to my house. Sandy had the forethought to take photos of my wounds. She would track the healing progress by taking pictures every week. It was encouraging to me to see how fast I was healing.

My toes, on the other hand, were not healing as well, or at all for that matter, and I was in pain. " I- need-more-Percoset" pain, 24 hours a day. What was my history with pain medication up to this point? I would take Tylenol, rarely, but it had to be a whopper of a headache. Here, in my present state, I was now singing the praises of Oxycodone. There were times when even the pain meds wouldn't touch it. I would just cry like a baby and beg for mercy from my God. I have known pain before, having birthed our children naturally at home, except for one. I never once asked for relief from the pangs of childbirth. My labors, most of them, were long. So I was well versed in the art of pain, or so I thought. This was different. Nerve pain in an extremity is very unique, "special" even.

About two weeks into this part of my journey, I had a person say to me, "You know how I handle pain?" "No, how?" I said hoping to hear this profound insight on how to endure this awful season in my life. "Well, I think happy thoughts," she said, clapping her hands together. "Oh," I said, "Like cuddly puppies and little girls in polka-dot dresses?" "Why, yes, you've got it." More clapping. Great. Eventually, I would learn to handle pain in the days ahead by taking the offensive. I would pray, sing, and shout praises to God. This was war and these were my weapons. If I was going down, I was not going to go quietly. So this woman was heading in right direction after all. However, mind over matter was not enough.

The use of SCDs had caused several clots in my legs, on the inside, just above the knees. These clots were discovered by ultra-sound. There was a concern that they would travel up my leg and hit my lungs. So the plan was to insert an IVC filter into the inferior vena cava. An IVC filter is a specially shaped mesh of very thin wires that acts like a strainer for your blood. This is placed in the vein to catch and stop blood clots from causing pulmonary embolism. Pulmonary embolism is when clots block blood vessels in your lungs, causing trouble breathing, chest pain, and, you guessed it – death. They explained the pros and cons, the risks that go with the procedure. Did I have a choice? Seeing those clots sitting in my veins on the ultra sound, I'd say no, I had no choice. Those SCDs were the "gift that just keeps on giving!"

There were two toes that were getting darker and darker until they were pitch black. They then began to shrivel up like prunes in the sun. I would fall asleep in a "Percoset stupor" to be awakened by stabbing pain in my feet as the drug would wear off. They were dying a slow death, way too slow. I was in my doc's office many times begging him to either take the toes off or put ME OUT OF MY MIS-ERY! My husband, ever optimistic, thought that just the very tips would have to come off. I was not sharing his positive outlook. I was tired. Exhausted by being in constant pain. I just wanted off this train. This was first of many times I would tell anyone who would listen, "Just shoot me."

Nearly a year and a half had passed since this whole ordeal began. As I lay there in my room one morning, I finally thought about this in realistic terms. This is not a bump in my road, this is major detour, a head on collision! No road signs, tumbleweed blowing and some road kill scattered here and there, just for effect. I have lost my way. Too many bad decisions. I can say with Dorothy, "Toto, I've the feeling we are not in Kansas anymore." Where am I, and how did I get here? I was used to being healthy and IF I became ill, I usually bounced back very quickly. I wasn't doing any bouncing this time. The only bouncing I was doing was from doctor to doctor.

Life around me was continuing. The farm was being run by my son Andrew, who lived nearby. The number of goats had to be pared down. We sold most of the milkers, just keeping two for fresh milk. Home schooling my son, Myles, was very sporadic. The older boys and Michael were trying to take up the slack, but they were very busy. Michael was working in Real Estate, and having done construction for years before we were married, he returned to the building trade. Michael was going straight-out all the time. We needed to keep ahead of the ever-mounting doctors bills. Fortunately, we had some savings and CD's we could cash in as well as other assets that we could liquidate. Michael was also my caregiver, dressing the wounds with a special anti-microbial ointment, "yellow goo" I called it. It was a special preparation made by the hospital. They had to be kept covered with bandages, after cleaning and slathering on the goo. This took an hour, twice a day. My husband is my hero! The care he gave me was so loving and kind. That man can find a funny side to anything, and HE DID!! Sometimes I'd be laughing so hard there were tears running down my face. He had this bandaging down to an art, so much so that he had to show the nurses how it was done. Sandy would come a couple times a week to check on the condition of the wounds. Never was there any sign of infection.

Thinking about those days is very difficult, the trauma of seeing my once healthy, beautiful body (God does not make junk. All our bodies are works of art) so marred was, and still is, very traumatic for me. The scar from the flesh peeling off my body remains painful to the touch. I cannot sleep on that side because of the pain, even six years later. The other bleed-outs left disfiguring scars everywhere. It was Michael's keen sense of humor, and the grace of God, that kept me in these dark times. He would allow me to express my feelings about my situation, but encouraged me to keep focused on my hope and my trust in God. Sometimes, when I was alone, I'd wail and cry out to God. Why was He allowing this? Yes, I know, the ol' proverbial, "Why, God?" I felt God was allowing me to emptied of everything.

12. Me and Job

I thought I had settled the issue of human personal trials, the why anyway, and who was the author of them. 26 years ago, we lost our daughter, Caitlin, to a crib death at 2 ½ months. She had become trapped under the playpen mattress when we were visiting family, and she wasn't in her regular crib. I didn't turn my back on God, but I was not talking much to Him. Who is this God that would take our daughter from us at such a young age? I obviously didn't really KNOW Him. It took me three years and a miscarriage to finally spur me into having a heart-to-heart with my "Papa." He had been telling me to read the book of Job. That's one book that you don't read for recreational purposes, or just a little light reading before bed. It is in the same category as Revelation. Job, now there was a guy who had real problems and heartaches. He lost all his children in a terrible accident, was stripped of all his livestock and then a strange illness, that caused wounds on his entire body. His "lovely" wife told him to "curse God and die." That was helpful. He was also surrounded with friends who pointed the finger, telling him he must have committed some serious sins to have such calamity befall him. With friends like that, who needs enemies? So, I read Job, finally. What I took away from my reading assignment was that God was not the perpetrator, or the cause of Job's trials. Job had an enemy that wanted to make an example of him. That enemy was Satan. Not every calamity, nor every trial, is the result of sin. Trials can stem from our living in a fallen world. In life, I believe, certain events can be seen as instructive tools. We can either yield and trust, thereby learning the intended lesson, or get mad and bitter and revisit this again at a later date. I was drinking of the cup that Job drank. Mine was just a sip compared to Job's. Job had, indeed, bowed the knee to fear. When all was intact and life was going smoothly, he feared losing everything. "For what I fear has come upon me, what I dread befalls me" (Job 3:25-26)

We have an enemy. Whether you recognize his presence or not, it does not change the fact of his existence. Our enemy is in the business of "killing, stealing and destroying." (John 10:10) I could, in every way, relate to that man of long ago. I had lost my daughter and now my body was covered with wounds. Yes, He allowed this suffering for a purpose or purposes. I believe for me, ONE purpose has been that I needed to see what I was made of. How deep my love for God went. Would I raise my fist heavenward against Him as Job's wife told him to do? Not a chance. I was passing the test, but hanging by a thread at times. I also remember praying that I wanted to know Him, REAL-LY KNOW Him. At that time of this prayer, I was feeling like I had merely scratched only the surface of who He was, "I want more Lord." Everyone has heard the saying, "Be careful what you pray for." Right? I think, it is in the valleys that we begin to realize who He is. His power, His love, His provision, grace and mercy! Yes, His mercy. I could have ended up a vegetable, or dead.

Testing does cause us, if we are willing, to go into "uncharted waters" in our beliefs. It can carry us into sometimes dark, deep waters where our feet no longer touch the bottom. The outcome depends on our reaction to the test. Do we humble ourselves or do we respond in pride or bitterness? I have always tried to NOT go into trials, faith's unknown territory, kicking and screaming, but I am not always successful. When things get really bad, I'm tempted to remind God that, "I'm not Mother Teresa."

My basic nature is one of a fighter. I never take something lying down. I was engaged in a great battle with an unseen enemy. This I saw as a fight to be fought, or in this case a donnybrook was more like it. I'd get knocked down and get right back up swinging. I caught glimpses of who my real enemy was and I knew he wanted me either dead or neutralized for good. Because of this understanding of the battle I was in, together with the very present grace of God and a loving family, I made it through. Even if you don't believe in God, there is a principle here that very worth considering. Everyone runs into trials. Do you get better or bitter? That's where the real battle is fought, in the recesses of our heart.

13. Bad Dream Turned Nightmare

What had been like life in a bad dream was about to turn into my worst nightmare. December 18, 2007, I woke up very early in the morning, about 4:30. I thought what woke me was that I needed to go to the bathroom. So I got up and walked awkwardly to the bathroom. On the way back, my walking was labored. It was hard to keep my concentration to get back to bed. I was very dizzy, and it scared me. I woke Michael and said, "Something is going on and I don't know what it is but I'm feeling pretty weird." He asked me if I thought he should call Dr. A? "Yes," I said, without a moment's hesitation. Doctor A. talked with me for a few minutes while I tried to describe what I was feeling. Unfortunately, his advice was, "Try and sleep a little more and if you're still not better, call me." I lay in my bed and we prayed…. About 6 am, I was feeling stranger than ever. Michael had fallen back asleep, and I woke him saying, "I think I'm having a stroke." Michael called Doctor A. again. He advised us to go to a hospital, half an hour away. Michael first called Doctor M., because she was the last doctor's appointment I'd had and she had prescribed yet another drug, Amicar. It was supposed to help me by keeping my body from having "bleed-outs." She knew immediately what the drug had done. "You're probably having a stroke. Go to the emergency room right away. I will call them and tell them that you're coming." (Stated in my hospital records was that the Amicar was the probable cause for my stroke.)

After a half an hour drive to the hospital, we were expecting the hospital to be ready for us. We were wrong. The waiting room was about 40 percent full, and we were told to wait until someone would call me in to do intake. After a while, a nice woman gestured to us and we were ushered into a small cubicle and given seats. Then, the drone of questions began. Billing questions, medical history questions. It took about 20 to 25 minutes. By the time she was finished, so was I. I could barely walk or talk. I needed a wheelchair to get to a bed in the treatment area. By this time, a throbbing pain was taking over in my head. What happened next is hard to wrap my head around, even to this day. Yet, considering my history with this hospital, it fits perfectly. They started an IV in my hand. They then proceeded to give me Prednisone, not t-PA. Tissue Plasminogen Activator, which according to some studies can often break up the clot and restore blood flow and prevent much permanent damage. If the stroke is past a certain point, three hours from the onset, they will administer Heparin. I was given neither. Prednisone was administered for at least an hour, until they took Michael seriously when he said, "She's getting worse." He had been sitting by my bed watching me slip further and further away. So they switched medications, (Plan A) but it was not before a lot of irreparable damage had been done. "Time lost is Brain lost," the commercial says, right? I don't know why they gave me Prednisone. My history of colitis was only briefly noted during intake. My symptoms, dizziness, not speaking clearly, and trouble walking, was screaming, "STROKE!" On top of the obvious symptoms, my doctor phoned ahead and told them I was coming in, and that I was having a stroke. How can this saga get any worse? Read on.

During intake, we told them I had been diagnosed with vasculitis, which calls for certain adjustments in the protocol of administration of drugs. The IV should have been placed in my leg/groin. Yet it was placed it in my hand. As I lay in a small room, machines humming on all sides, my hand started hurting, and yes, it was turning black. I began waving my hand to get my husband's attention, to show him I was in pain, and that my hand was discoloring. By this time, I could not speak and I was just barely lucid. Michael called the doctor, who came quickly and realized what was happening. The nurse/technician that started the IV SHOULD HAVE been instructed by the attending physician where to place the IV, since my diagnosis of vasculitis was in the chart. People make mistakes. I get that. But all of them on me?? This is why my husband calls my story "the perfect storm." The strange convergence of incomprehensible circumstances coming together to create this, what I call a "train wreck." Most circumstances were the drugs that were given to me and the rest was human error. Think I could qualify for the "poster child" for medical mishaps? But...if I had been a little more out of it, I COULD HAVE LOST MY WHOLE HAND, on my left side, the WORKING side of my body. God's mercy was all over me.

The doctor applied nitro glycerin to my hand at my husband's suggestion (we had been this route earlier with my feet), and it worked. My hand started to return to normal, except for my pinky finger, the top half of which remained black. They moved the IV to my groin, and finally began to administer the proper medication for someone suffering a stroke.

How long is Satan's leash? He was going in for the kill.

14. My Last Rites

When I was once again conscious, Father Glen from a local Anglican church was praying over me the Prayer of Last Rites. I was listening for what seemed like a long while before I opened my eyes. "This can't be good," I remember thinking. I was just lying there listening and smiling – at least I thought I was. I was scowling because one half of my face refused to work. Nothing was working on my right side, least of all that side of my face. My whole right side was completely paralyzed. My brain was no longer making the connection to that side of my body.

Michael came in the room after Father Glen left and welcomed me back to the "land of the living." I didn't know how long I was unconscious, but I was thinking, "What am I still doing here?" It had been about 24 hours since my arrival to the ER.

My next memory was of me asking Michael, by gesturing, for something to eat. I could think thoughts in my head, but I could not get them from my brain to my mouth. My stroke had completely wiped out my ability to speak. I could not even remember HOW to speak.

Prior to the stroke, my diet was very limited. Now, I didn't remember the restrictions I had lived under before. So I motioned to Michael to get me what he had, a doughnut and coffee. Neither of us was knowledgeable about what happens with a stroke survivor and the inability to swallow liquids, never mind a doughnut. Ignorance is bliss. Michael gave me a bite of his doughnut and a sip of coffee. OHHHH, yes…. I wanted my own. I was very hungry, so he hurried to the cafeteria and bought me a doughnut and a decaf coffee. It was wonderful! I didn't think twice about it, I had no problems because I was taking my time, savoring it. Later that day, the doctor order a "swallow test." Oops, didn't they know I had already run that "test?" Call it an "independent study" and I had passed with flying colors.

My boys came to see me, a couple at a time. My inability to speak was very frustrating. Find me a woman who can't speak and I'll show you frustration. It was so good to see their faces, even if their names escaped me. For the life of me, I could not remember their names. Come to think of it, they were used to it. When they were young, I would want to call one of them and would go through the whole list, even occasionally, throwing in one of our dog's names. When they complained, I promised to pay for counseling. "That's life in a big family," I'd tell them. I remembered Michael's name, at least.

According to the American Stroke Association statistics, about 795,000 Americans each year suffer a new or have a recurrent stroke. On average there is a stroke happening every 40 seconds, with one out of 18 deaths blamed on stroke. That is about 137,000 people a year. It is the number four cause of death in America today, and sixty percent of those are female. It seems to me that everyone knows someone who's had a stroke.

There are three types of strokes, and ischemic was the kind I suffered. Then there are hemorrhagic, and TIAs or transient ischemic attack. A TIA is a warning event that speaks of bad things to come. It is the proverbial "shot across the bow." The person who has such an event should be checked right away. Usually there is no damage or lasting effects from a TIA.

Ischemic strokes have the same outcome, even though they are caused by two different issues in the body. Clots that form in a blocked blood vessel are referred to as thrombotic. Embolic clots forms somewhere in the body and then travels to the brain where they can lodge in the narrowing blood vessels. This cuts off the blood supply to the portion of the brain beyond the clot causing death of surrounding brain cells.

Hemorrhagic stroke is when a blood vessel bursts, causing bleeding in the brain. This floods the cranium with blood and causes brain cells to die. There are many self-induced factors that cause strokes, everything from obesity, high blood pressure, poor diet, smoking, high cholesterol, and inflammation.

It occasionally grips me, the thought that IF my physician had not told me to wait two hours that morning. IF I had been seen right away in the ER and not required to do intake that took almost 30 minutes. IF I had been given the correct medication immediately, how many of my abilities would I still have today? So much time was lost, and brain was lost, due to a multitude of bad decisions and mistakes. Again, I felt like a pawn in my own life story. I believe that the hospital mistakes sealed my fate. Their errors caused the effects imposed on my hand/arm, which basically no longer function. The drop foot that makes walking without a brace impossible.

The rest of my stay in the hospital was spent assessing the damage done by the ischemic stroke. I was weak as a newborn kitten, could not speak and could not walk. A nurse brought me a dry erase board to write messages so that I could communicate. I would have needed to be able to spell and I could not spell the simplest of words. I could shake my head "yes" and "no" and I frequently got that mixed up. I was exhausted all the time. All I wanted to do was sleep. I was trapped in this body at age 50, captive to the ravages of this cruel taskmaster called stroke. Life as I was knew it, was over.

15. Inmate at Rehab Facility

The days in the hospital, following my stroke are a bit fuzzy. All I remember is doctors coming and going into my room and sleeping in between visitors. The doctors started a trend that seemed to stick with me well after my stroke, into recovery and beyond. I was no longer a "thinking person," so they thought. I was to be talked *about*, not talked *to*. They would come into the room, with the young doctors in training and discuss me, as though I were a "thing." I had the desire to communicate. What woman wouldn't? It appeared that everyone assumed that mentally there was very little "upstairs," because I could not speak. To this day, because I walk "stupid," so stupid, I must be. Because I have trouble speaking, especially when I'm tired, I'm mentally missing some marbles. All of a sudden, I was catapulted into this group of people that are seen as *less than*, or not *all there* as a result of surviving a stroke. Usually stroke survivors are older, wiser adults. What an insult.

I recall on one occasion, a couple of years post-stroke, I was talking with a gentleman about Real Estate. The conversation wandered into some more technical aspects of it, discussing capital gains and so on. This gentleman was quite astonished, and didn't disguise it, that I was able to carry on a conversation at this "level." Not only was I blonde, but I'd had a stroke, and he was amazed! Even to this day, six years past my stroke, people still have a hard time believing my mind works better than my leg. When I'm going to my car in the parking lot of the grocery store, I have been known to laugh and comment to people who stare at me, "Don't worry, I drive better than I walk."

The strong suggestion of my group of MD's was that I go to rehab at a separate facility, still related to the hospital. The rehab was a nice facility, very institutional in appearance, but fairly new. It was clean and fresh looking. At $5,000.00+ a week, my husband was hoping it would be worth the cost if they could help in my recovery in a significant way. At $5,000+ a week, (that's five days, not seven days) it should have looked like resort/spa in the Bahamas, complete with five-star rooms, chocolates on the pillows, and champagne in the mini fridge. I should be walking and talking in no time! I was transported to the building by ambulance, not limousine. That should have my first clue as to what to expect. I remember how getting out in the fresh winter air was so wonderful! I would have loved to stay outside a little longer. So normal! Something I was now always in search of even though, at the time, I couldn't define that need. Normal was seriously lacking at rehab. For me it was just another chapter in my nightmare.

My appearance had an uncanny resemblance to a concentration camp survivor, or a New York runway model without make-up. At 103 pounds, I weighed what I did at age 11. I had gone from 135 pounds, a size 11-12 to a size 4. Sandy, my friend, brought me some nice clothes to wear, fancy sweats, judging my new size exactly. God bless her for her kindness and thoughtfulness. The first morning in my new digs, the aide came in to wake me up. She told me to get up and dressed, and that she would help get me to the bathroom. The burly young woman tossed my clothes at me, and they landed next to me on the bed. I was so weak I could barely get up, never mind dress myself. This one-handed living was going to take some getting used to. I looked at my shirt and just said to myself "Now what?" I could not figure out how to put on my shirt, or how to do it one-handed. When I didn't take the cue to get myself dressed, she sighed heavily (like I was a reticent child who needed a good "guilt trip" to motivate me), and began to undress and then dress me in my day clothes. She was well-versed in dressing one-armed people; it was all new to me. I was helped into my wheelchair and taken to the bathroom. She helped me every step of the way and then helped me wash up for breakfast. I felt we were contestants in a game show and I expected that I would hear an ear-piercing buzzer any second." Time's up. You lose!" There was no conversation, no encouragement, just MOVE!

I was very unaccustomed to being treated in such a manner, never having been so helpless before. It was an awful feeling. Again, I was a "thing," not a person worthy of respect. I was being reduced to nothing more than a shell of a human being, who now was not supposed to feel like I was worth anything or had no right to expect more. The place I was in mentally, emotionally, was a very vulnerable one and folks were "writing on my page" daily. Those emotional wounds didn't heal for a long time. Even recalling that time arouses a sick feeling in the core of my being.

Then we went to the dining area where, I was wheeled to a table and left there to wait for my breakfast. Despite having eaten a cake doughnut the morning after my stroke, Doctor's orders were to keep me on a soft food diet for three days. Before I could eat solids, they would run another swallow test. For the life of me, neither my husband nor I can recall what it was they gave me, but I do remember being very hungry for the first few days. I was given the "swallow test" at the end of three days and it was decided that I COULD handle soft foods, which did NOT include cake doughnuts.

My fellow patients were in various stages of recovery. A few were happy, but most were sullen and would not interact with anyone or make eye contact. I do remember one dear elderly woman who was always spreading joy and love to us all. She was the "Bob Hope" of rehab. Even though I could not reply, she'd wheel over to my wheelchair and tell me "Everything is going to be alright, honey," that it was "All up-hill from here". She would find me every morning, come over and smile saying, "It is going to get better, honey". God bless this woman.

After meals, when I wasn't slotted to do rehab, which was twice a day for an hour, I was forced to sit in my wheelchair in the hall, alone. I could not go to my room and sleep, something I desperately wanted to do. So I sat in the hall and, usually, cried. Crying was something that came so easily. Tears would start at the drop of a hat. I would sit there trying to understand, HOW the hell did I get here, and how do I get out!

My husband came every day, staying for as long as he could, and my boys came, too, in between their work schedules. Michael had to run the house, and keep our six-year-old Myles, and 14-year-old Sam, on schedule, plus earn a living to keep us afloat financially. When word got out about my stroke, friends brought meals for the guys.

At rehab, I felt like an inmate in a prison. I wanted to leave the first morning I was there. Only a few people were polite and kind, and treated the patients with respect. I was so weak, there was little I could do in the way of exercise for my legs. We worked some on my hand and arm.

The most useful part of my time there was speech therapy. I was given sheets with pictures on them, the kind that you would give a 2-year-old learning to talk. My job was to say the words when the therapist pointed to one of the pictures, or just go down the sheet saying the words a fast as I could. One of the exercises was flash cards with simple math problems, like 2+2. I could not add 1+1 never mind 2+2. Nothing was "flashing" in my brain. Doing math was like trying reach down into my memory bank which, as of yet, was not "on line." I was no longer able to do the simplest math. If ever I was smug about ANY of my abilities, they were all gone. It is near impossible to pull off "smug" when you're drooling. All of us have forgotten an item on a shopping list, or where you put those darn car keys, your mom's birthday. Hey, it happens, right? Me, I was forgetting to swallow. No wonder people talked at me like I was just a "thing," I thought to myself, wiping my chin.

I was exhausted by these mental gymnastics. I needed sleep, but it was not allowed during the day. I have since learned that sleep is very good for a brain that has suffered a stroke. Sleep helps in the healing of the cells that are working to repair themselves. Apparently the staff at rehab, didn't know that, or more likely, it was too inconvenient. Retrieving each patient from our beds to do rehab was just not efficient or convenient.

There was a device they strapped me into that was to assist me in walking. There was no way I could stand on my own. So we would spend 15 minutes getting strapped into the harness, five to seven minutes simulating walking, then another ten minutes getting free of the harness. I was spent when it was all over.

After dinner we were then allowed to retreat to our "cells" for the night. Most would watch the television that each room had. Michael would drive the half hour back in the evenings to spend a few hours with me, sometimes bringing Myles and Sam. It was never long enough, the time would fly by and it would be the end of visiting hours. I very much wanted to go home with them.

Then it would start. In the wee hours of the night there would be blood curdling screams, like there was torture going on somewhere in the bowels of the building. I don't know why, but it was even harder to hear men screaming. Either way, sleep didn't come easily. If we had been allowed to close our doors at night, it would have gone along way to muffling the nighttime "torture sessions."

16. Against Medical Advice

On the third day, Michael came in the morning and asked me if I wanted come home. I burst out crying in answer to his question. He needed no interpretation, no sign language or visuals. YES! I want to go home! He saw the way I and others were being treated; he wanted me out as bad as I did. My tears in response to the question were all the answer he needed. Michael went home that evening and began to prepare the house for my return. I was so happy; my husband was going to spring me from this "joint." All the doctors advised against my going home so early. I would need help with everything, and they said I needed "expert" care. I thought it had been "expert care" that got me here! Michael was fully capable and willing to learn any helpful hints for my being cared for at home. He was the one who had successfully seen to my wounds for months while they were healing. So, Against Medical Advice, I was going home. Michael planned to take time off from work, one month that turned into three. But who was counting.

Up to now, we had done most every thing *advised* by the doctors. It was medical advice that caused the stroke, the injuries of two toes, my fingertip, and the wounds all over my body, coupled with the mistakes in the ER that almost killed me. It was time to take back the reins. A little late, but we were not going waste time bemoaning the place in which we found ourselves. There would plenty of time for reflection later, much later. Michael bought a Porta-Potty for all of our convenience, as I was too weak to walk to the bathroom and I would need help every time I went. He cleaned the bedroom "stem to stern." Fresh, clean bedding was put on the bed, and the house given a thorough cleaning. That day could not come soon enough. We had to wait for the doctors to do a final evaluation, and to show my husband how to pick me up and move me safely from wheelchair to bed and back again. So after five days at rehab, they released me to my husband's care. I felt like I was breaking out of jail as we pulled away. I never wanted to look back. It felt so good to put that place in my rear view mirror!!

17. Home to the Farm

I was going home to my own bed! I wanted to able to look out the window and see our horses in our pastures. I wanted to see the rolling hills behind our barn where my boys spent winter days sledding. I wanted to be in my familiar, NOT antiseptic, HOME! On my own schedule, to sleep whenever I wanted to, eat when and what I wanted to eat. Michael borrowed a lightweight wheelchair that would maneuver easily in our house. We all forgot that we would need a ramp to get me and my chair into the house. We improvised. Michael and my oldest son, Jedidiah, did the ceremonial "Queen of Sheba" carry, chair and all, to get up the stairs and in the house.

I felt so sorry for those I left behind, the night screamers, the men and women stuck there obviously unhappy, depressed. One of the counselors at rehab had said to me "Don't be surprised if you get depressed after such a life altering event as a stroke." Thank God I got out of there as quickly as I did. Staying there, THAT would be depressing! I would deal with depression in the days ahead, however, as what had happened finally dawned on me. So few of the people who worked there were kind and respectful. That's got to take its toll on a person's spirit. I wish I could have led a jail break for everyone.

I had no idea that I was not going recover completely, not that this would have changed how hard I worked. I had no idea how much work it was going to take to get me where I am today. One thing I did know for certain was that home was where my healing would begin. Home, where I was surrounded with love and laughter, and good food!

My speech therapist, sneaked practice sheets in my bag as I was leaving. She told me, "If you do these every day, you'll see, it will begin to get easier and easier. Don't give up." The only word that rolled off my tongue with ease was "no." By the time I was home for a week, I

Now, put those two words together and it's not
my husband. We had a good laugh about that.
ne thing. Everyone, in their own way, brought
m would do charades with me trying to figure
at at mealtime. One day, he was stumped when
dessert. We were laughing so hard, by the time
was, my sides ached, tears rolling down my
ıg to look at the funny side to everything; it
helped all of us take this season in stride. What I didn't like was everyone waiting on me. It was so difficult to just lie there while everyone
scurried around. One day, it occurred to me, all I can do well is point!

It was sometimes very hard to see anything happy about my circumstances. Also, I was in a lot of pain. The wounded toes were still
"pruning up." My pinky finger was yelling at me constantly as the tip
self-amputated. The reality of what had happened had not completely had its full impact on me yet. I was too consumed with the here and
now to get a birds eye view of my life and what the implications were
for the future.

I have no intention of suggesting that, at times, tensions didn't run
high. The financial strain was underlying the fabric of everyday life.
We were being sued by the hospital (for maiming and nearly killing
me.) All our savings were gone. Michael was trying to take care of me
and work two professions. Many times we were living off our credit
cards to buy groceries. There were so many claims to the money
Michael was earning, and it was very stressful. Michael tried to keep
the financial picture hidden from me as long as possible. As my brain
healed and re-engaged, I became more aware of our financial condition, and it wasn't a pretty picture. We could not afford the intensive
therapy that is so needed the first year. Looking back, the $5000.00
spent at rehab, would have been better spent at a local rehab facility
when I was four to five months out from my stroke. There were
things that would have helped my journey back to functioning physi-
cally, that I could not do at home. Despite our financial drama, God
did have at my disposal a handful of people who were going help me
on my way to recovery.

18. How Do I Fix This?

Four months post-stroke, I was starting to read again, although I had trouble focusing on particular lines. It was as though the words were jumping around on the page. I ordered from Amazon every book I could find written by people who had had strokes. Many of them were used and I paid $1 for them. I was desperate to learn how to fix this "problem." My personality had always been that, whenever something confronts me, ANY problem, I go into hyper gear to learn all there is to learn how to fix it, not just cope with it. I went back to my herb book and found the specific brain/nerve healing herbs. Then, I ordered the tinctures that help heal the brain. I felt that I had lost the bulk of ready-knowledge that used to be always easily recalled for any health situation. It was like starting from scratch, and was very disheartening. But, I now knew 1+1 =2. After a couple of months, even some of the multiplication tables were retuning. I hoped it was just matter of time and I would gain what I had before in other areas.

I was devouring every book about what others did for rehab, researching where I could access the same tools. I tried everything but stem cell injections. I wanted my body back! I, by God's design, assembled a team of specialists to help me work my way back, as close as I could get, to my former self. Many of these people I knew before my stroke and they were my friends. Imagine knowing so many loving, talented people that were ready and willing to see me through this difficult time. This is a comprehensive list of what I have done.

MASSAGE WITH EMPHASIS ON CRANIAL SACRAL

I will start with my massage therapist. Brandy Stevens, who also does Cranial Sacral therapy, would come to my home and work wonders on my poor, ravaged body. With half my body dragging, I constantly was out of alignment, and by gentle massage, and sometimes not so gentle..... she would loosen the tight, rigid muscles, or what is usually referred to as spasticity and I would find relief. Brandy would work on me sometimes for three hours; often I would sleep through most of it. The cranial sacral part of my massage was always gentle, subtle, but nonetheless powerful in results. Cranial Sacral Therapy seeks to restore the natural position of the bones and to release compression in the head and neck area. This type of massage, freed other areas of my body to heal because it opened up communication lines from my brain to every area of my body.

Brandy coming to my home, increased the benefits of our time together because it allowed me to just be still afterward, letting the results of her work, make a more lasting impression. When Brandy moved to Colorado, I began to look for another massage therapist that was trained in CST. God, being who He is, found me Gloria Kozura, who was of the same mind, never in a hurry and equally as gifted at her calling. She also went above and beyond in many ways. I am so grateful for these women.

One very debilitating result from stroke is spasticity. Spasticity is caused by damage or injury to the part of the central nervous system that controls voluntary movement. This damage disrupts signals between the nervous system and muscles. It is this imbalance that increases muscle activity or spasms.

Spasticity can make movement, the way one carries themselves, and balance difficult. It may affect your ability to move one or more of your limbs. There are times when, spasticity is so severe that it gets in the way of daily activities. For me, massage is what works best to manage the small amount that I have. It may strike at anytime. There are different stimuli that cause me to temporarily lose control of my affected side. Putting on or taking off my coat or shirt cause my right side to stiffen. But unlike some survivors, the spasm lets go in a minute or two. Botox is a temporary solution for spasticity. One application in an effected area can, relieve muscle rigidness for about three months.

Cranial Sacral was one of the many therapies I explored for healing my body and I had amazing results! I spent one week at Upledger

Institute in Florida, whose specialty is Cranial Sacral Therapy. We stayed at my in-law's winter home about 40 minutes away. For three hours in the morning and two and a half in the afternoon, I had no less than two, usually three, therapists working on me at one time. Acupuncture was also part of their regimen at Upledger. I got more results out of one hour at Upledger than I did one week at rehab. Everyone was so very kind. I went there six months after my stroke. I walked in there dependent on a four-prong walker and I returned home, able to walk without any assistance. I still use my cane outside on uneven ground. And, I keep it close by so if I need to keep someone in line, man or beast, it is wonderful "tool/weapon." So our Boer buck found out when he started to push me around in the barn one day. He may have nasty horns, but I have a cane, and I know how to use it! The dizziness that plagued me was greatly diminished and my balance was much better. Here's a brief explanation of Cranial Sacral:

"Few structures have as much influence over the body's ability to function properly as the brain and spinal cord that make up the central nervous system. And, the central nervous system is heavily influenced by the cranial sacral system – the membranes and fluid that surround, protect and nourish the brain and spinal cord" Using a soft touch which is generally no greater than 5 grams – about the weight of a nickel – practitioners release restrictions in the soft tissues that surround the central nervous system. CST is increasingly used as a preventive health measure for its ability to bolster resistance to disease and it's effective for a wide range of medical problems associated with pain and dysfunction." My time spent at Upledger was healing in several ways. Having practitioners work on me for so long everyday, I "felt the love," very different from rehab. The effects their efforts had on me were over and above my expectations. I felt that emotional healing was continued in that setting. I was given time think about the place I found myself and really begin the process of grieving, and the whole gambit of emotions that went with it. Several times while they were working on me, a torrent of tears would come flowing out, like someone turned on a faucet. It was like an eruption from the depths of my soul. I would try not to cry because of the feeling that I was out of control, out of MY control. It would not be stopped or stuffed. However, they made feel that it was a safe place. I

began the grieving process in the company these gentle, kind healers. I would love to return for another week someday.
* Upledger.com

PHYSICAL THERAPY

I am so thankful for my friend, Michele Bessette, who is a physical therapist. She would come to my house and teach me ways to strengthen what I had left in my leg and arm. Michelle left me with exercises that I could do on my own everyday. It was so helpful. One exercise that I still do now is, holding on to the sink and doing squats. Sometimes I would "workout" (kind of a strong word for what I was doing, but it's all relative) twice a day. My motto had always been "If some is good-more must be better." Michele is a farming friend from long before my stroke, so she knew me before and after. Never did I feel any of these women were "lording" over my fallen state. There was no condescension, just pure love, and desire to help my journey move along. Occasionally, I came into contact with those who would treat me in a "less than" manner or made feel they were alpha women, for the sole reason that I was "broken." I would keep them from returning. I was so obviously wounded in body, but what probably what was a greater wound was the crushing of my spirit, feeling like my heart was broken in small pieces that would take a lot of time to put me back together again. Experience told me the need to protect my heart and spirit from anyone writing on the pages of either.

Back in 1989, when I was delivering my fourth child, the mid-wife, all through the delivery, made many very disparaging remarks, as though I was "doing it all wrong." There are very few times when a woman is more vulnerable than when she's giving birth. I felt so bad, heavy-hearted, after the birth. This bully of a woman, wrote on my page and something had to be done. Six weeks after the delivery, I went to visit her, if for nothing else but to look her in the eye, and declare how great the delivery was. "Setting the record" straight. Needless to say, I found another mid-wife for child number five.

The healing of my heart, my spirit, and emotions, was just as critical an element to my recovery, maybe more so. Having the stroke reduced me in so many ways, seen and unseen.

ACCUPUNCTURE

I went to an acupuncturist that was said to be very gifted in his abilities. When we met, he was very encouraged by doing some pulse readings on me. By tuning into the sensations beneath one's fingertips, at six small positions along a single artery, part of what's being read is the patient's entire subtle body bio-field. My understanding is that he was listening to my body's ebb and flow, to see if the connections were weak or strong. Very similar, I think, to Cranial Sacral Therapy where one listens/feels the flow of the fluids, reaction to touch, and the rigidity or free-flowing normal movement in the cranium. There are some skeptics that say it is ridiculous, and then there are practitioners that can accurately read the bodies systems and their history and prove their finding with medical tests. I decided to do acupuncture because of testimonies of positive outcomes.

Dr. P. felt I would be able to make real gains in my recovery under his care. I always felt that he cared and was fully committed to seeing me regain as much as possible. Since a majority of acupuncture points are either connected to or are located near neural structures, suggests that acupuncture stimulates the nervous system. I was dealing with pain as well as the interruption of the signals from my brain, to my limbs on my right side.

Acupuncture is used to treat a myriad of problems. Studies have shown that acupuncture may help in the rehabilitation of stroke patients. So, I thought it was worth a try.

After about six sessions, Doctor P. suggested my recovery was being hindered by me; that what he was doing should have had significant effect on me. I was noticing diminished pain, particularly in my arm and shoulder. I was sleeping more soundly, feeling rested in the morning. He thought that there was something emotionally holding my body in this place, a blockage of sorts and unless this was taken care of, there was little more he could do. We met a few more times and, because it seemed to be doing less than we both expected, we decided to end the sessions. In the defense of this modality, it was a while until I realized how wounded I was in spirit and emotions. Later on I found myself needing to forgive the "players" in my drama. That may have been the reason for the blockage. I was holding a lot of anger towards some of my physicians and the hospital for their many blunders.

THE FELDENKRAIS METHOD

The Feldenkrais Method, developed by Moshe Feldenkrais, is an educational system that teaches the body to move and function more efficiently and comfortably. Its goal is to re-educate the nervous system and improve motor ability. By manipulating and imitating the limbs natural movements, you are able to re-train that part of the body to correct its function. I was not fully convinced something so subtle would work. He would take my leg and foot to teach it how to hit the ground correctly. This did amazing things for my gait. It retrained my brain to take the muscle capabilities I had left and maximize them. In the right shoes, I can walk less like a lumbering giant. The most valuable response my body had was, less pain in my legs and feet. I had access to one of the premier Feldenkrais instructors, Keith Johnson. He is so gifted!

REFLEXOLOGY

A reflexologist and personal friend, Julia Pomeroy, was able to target specific areas of my body through massage of my feet. Julia was able bring most my body's functions and organs, back to normal. On the soles of our feet are different zones that relate to every organ, or area in our bodies. For example, one issue that was always a problem was my eyes and keeping them open. My eye lids felt like they weighed a ton all the time. Just in passing, I shared this with her during one appointment and she went right to work. When she was done it was so much better, and subsequent sessions improved and eventually alleviated the problem altogether. Also my gallbladder was showing signs of stress. Surprise! Within two months, it was nearly normal. At least I STILL HAD A GALLBLADDER!!

I was so grateful, and still am to this day, for the love and care Julia showed me, and the fact that she was willing to come to my home. She would start every session with a foot soak, using essential oils in the water. It was a sweet journey into relaxation and peace every time. Reflexology is intended to alleviate stress and help the body achieve a state of deep relaxation and homeostasis, in other words the balance of the body's biochemical and other systems. The sessions were beginning to maintain their effects longer and longer, one treatment building up on another. I felt like a "peaceful hunk of putty" when we finished each time. Coming out of a season that was riddled with discomfort and pain, it was so healing in many ways.

CHIROPRACTIC

Dr. Chad Hawk, was my chiropractor and knew me prior to my stroke. When Michael and I were being sued by the hospital and our cash reserves were very low, Chad never charged me for his services. There was no way I could have availed myself of the desperately needed adjustments if I had had to pay for them. As I was beginning to walk again and because half of my body was on "vacation," my left side had to work really hard. This inequity threw my back out of alignment frequently. Sometimes it would disable me altogether. I would be unable to even get up from my bed. A few times, Chad would drive 40 minutes to my house to "straighten me out." He had a very unique approach, not the usual "Linda Blair" (from the Exorcist), twisting your head as though you were an owl. Or sitting on you and twisting your body into a pretzel. He was gentle and specific, as though he was coaxing the body to right itself. It never failed to work. His specialty is working with the upper cervical, and the atlas, the upper back and the bones at the base of the head. OR, in his words, "I am a tonal upper cervical chiropractor MC2 and Relational Chiropractic Technique with a strong backing in Blair,(not Linda) HIO, Toggle Recoil) with a tonal full spine analysis and use Thompson, Network, Torque Release, Diversified...anything the person needs for the adjustment." I'm sure that speaks volumes to some reading this. To me this translated into, "a lot of tricks in his bag."

Dizziness was occasionally a problem, especially the first two years. Chad was very good at gently freeing the bones in my head that had "locked up" and would cause the swimming feeling that accompanied that miss-alignment. Each time he'd adjust me, it held longer and longer. Now, I have none of the dizziness that plagued me. Chiropractic care, given by a GOOD chiropractor is ESSENTIAL for recovery following a stroke.

HYPERBARIC CHAMBER

Hyperbaric Oxygen Treatment, HBOT, is one of the most powerful devices that can be used post stroke. The sooner that it is applied, the better chance you have for healing the damaged cells in your brain.

I had access to a hyperbaric chamber, because very kind group of families who have autistic children shared theirs with me. Now I have one at home, thanks to Michael's family and my mom giving us the funds to purchase one. Here's how hyperbaric works:

"Hyperbaric oxygen works to improve stroke and TBI patients by repairing and generating new blood vessels to the injured parts of the brain. Once the ischemic tissues no longer suffer from a lack of oxygen, they are able to begin to repair the injured neurons, glial cells and extracellular matrix. The generation of new blood vessels occurs as a direct result of daily hyperbaric oxygen treatments. This does not occur with pure oxygen at normal atmospheric pressures. The number of treatments required varies for each individual but in my experience the best results occur when at least 60 daily treatments are done. If only 20 to 30 treatments are done, the patient will often experience "backsliding" and may lose some of the improvement they gained from the hyperbaric oxygen treatments. In addition, some patients will not even begin to improve until they have had more than 30 or 40 treatments."*

I used the chamber as often as I could, usually everyday, sometimes twice a day. After about 40 dives I began to notice significant improvements in speech, and the ability to hold a thought in my head for more than a second. My hearing and balance improved. They weren't perfect but better.

At first, I would go in the tank and, being somewhat claustrophobic, asked my husband to sit by the chamber while I was in it. Then, after a number of successful dives, I began to look at it as my get-away. I would read, work on my computer, exercise or just sleep. I was soon soloing it, so Michael would not have to sit by the tank anymore.

In every developed country in Europe, HBOT is a STANDARD part of rehab. The sooner it's applied, the better the recovery outcomes. There are, springing up all over America, stand-alone clinics, that just do hyperbaric oxygen treatments. It is used for MS, Autism, Lyme Disease, traumatic brain injury including strokes, and more. You can even rent a chamber to use in your home. It is well worth it!

* http://www.tldp.com/issue/180/Hyperbaric%20Oxygen.html
http://www.medlink.com/medlinkcontent.asp

TOTAL GYM

Next, is my Total Gym, which I did not get until 3 ½ years had gone by. I wish I had known about this device earlier. This is a great way to strengthen your core. I don't know how else to say this, but I tip over a lot. I don't necessarily have to be moving to bring this about. When I faithfully use the gym, I notice a big difference in posture and my core strength and I tip less. My legs and arms have greater mobility and strength. There are many ways to adjust the settings to attain a safe workout equal to your capabilities. There is absolutely no resemblance to the way I use it and how spokesperson for Total Gym, Christie Brinkley, does it. None.

DEALING WITH DROP-FOOT

Immediately after my stroke, I was confined to a wheelchair, and warned that the likelihood of walking again, was pretty slim. (" Peanut butter! Peanut butter!") At four+ months I was able to stand for longer periods of time. That's when I knew, I was going walk, and I "ditched" the wheelchair. I was introduced to the AFO brace. A plastic molded splint, the fit very uncomfortably in my shoes. I HATED THAT THING. It was like wearing a sign that said, "I AM HAND-ICAPPED." I wore it for two years, modifying it some by having my husband cut the foot section back to the heel. This modification, allowed a more fluid stride, but still kept my foot from dragging. There are some expensive models that have hinged ankle, that are supposed to allow more free-flowing stride. I put up with the AFO for a while, but started researching other ways of dealing with my "sleeping" foot. I found a great option. Because my ankle was still fairly flexible, with minimal spasticity, I was able to use the X-Strap, or Dorsi-Strap system. Early on, I found that wearing a night-splint, coupled with regular stretching, kept my ankle fairly supple. The Dorsi-Strap consists of straps that tie to your lace-up shoes. Then the straps wrap around a cuff on the ankle, pulling up the foot. I call it a winch to keep the wench's foot up. The straps use Velcro, which secures the straps tightly on the cuff. That's the only Velcro that I will allow on my body. You can buy the lace straps separately, and just use the same cuff with any shoe. The straps and cuffs come in three different colors. The straps are available in two widths. I found that the thin straps cut in to my ankle, making it very uncomfortable for any length of time. This ingenious way of dealing with foot drop, has afforded me a little bit of "normalcy," the AFO brace did not. Most people don't even know I am wearing it, even when I wear shorts.

A CANE FOR EVERY OCCASION

I always thought that a cane is just a cane. Not true. If you don't need a cane, BRAVO! But, if you are like me, and might tip over by simply turning your head too quickly, use the cane. Still, why would anyone want to wear a sign that says "ATTENTION: I am Handicapped?" If you want to see what I'm talking about, go look at what they are selling at the drug store. Just recently I noticed that our local drug store has finally begun to update the options. However, even "stylish" does not necessarily mean "better."

When you are going shopping, you need a cane that will hook over your arm, or a strap that will keep it on your wrist. While you are looking at an item of clothing, a rump roast, etc., you don't have to hold the cane. Nothing screams, "I'm handicapped," louder than a cane continually dropping on the ground. You'd be surprised to hear how many uses I have found for a cane with a hook. Last summer, I drew water with a bucket from the pond for my garden, which was planted by the edge of Arlington Pond. Saved me from dragging a hose around all summer.

If you are going out to dinner, you want a slim, pretty cane, preferably neutral in color, or better yet, matching your outfit. If you are heading to a sports event, you need a rugged, but stylish, one. This summer, my youngest son, Myles, played baseball. To get to the field, I had to make my way down a steep hill. A "Hurry Cane," is perfect for such an occasion. The tip has a swivel that allows it to make contact with the ground, no matter what the angle. When a family member makes a comment about my five canes, I just say, "Hey, I'm accessorizing!"

OTHER THERAPIES

Therapies that I have explored are the Bioness and Tailwind. The Tailwind unit attaches to a table top and the subject does repetitive motion to retrain the mind. " *The Tailwind is arm rehabilitation exercise device that has been shown in scientific studies to improve arm function and range of motion in people with partial paralysis. It requires no installation or technical expertise. Developed by researchers at the University of Maryland Medical School, Tailwind can help you regain lost arm function after stroke, traumatic brain injury, cerebral palsy, and other brain injuries. With The Tailwind arm exercise device stroke survivors and others can recover the life they thought was lost forever.*"*

It is said of this therapy, that results are favorable even years after a stroke occurs. In other words, it is never too late. I contacted Tailwind and offered to try their device as a guinea pig, of sorts, and if the device worked on my sleeping arm, I'd be their best spokesperson! I've networked now with a number of rehab facilities, physicians and physical therapists, I'd get the word out. They did not buy it. You can't blame a girl for trying.

How Tailwind Therapy Works. Seated at a table, the user moves two handles along resistance-free tracks, to the rhythm of an auditory cue. After repeated exercise sessions, the user will be able to move his affected arm farther and farther out along the track. The Tailwind utilizes a "sound-to-brain" neural pathway retraining method to help survivors of partial paralysis achieve life-altering results." Cost of the device $2500.00.

The other therapy that was intriguing, but very costly, was Bioness. This first piece of information is for drop foot: *"The system delivers electrical stimulation in a precise sequence, which then activates the muscles to lift the foot to take a step. The result may be a more natural walking pattern (gait) combined with enhanced stability and confidence"* Bioness also has a hand/arm rehabilitation device. *"The H200 Wireless Hand Rehabilitation System stimulates the appropriate nerves and muscles of the forearm and hand and helps to reeducate weak or paralyzed muscles." "The system applies electrical stimulation in a precise sequence, which then activates the muscles. This helps the muscles relearn to respond to signals for movement" "The orthosis fits to your forearm and wrist, and communicates wirelessly with the control unit. Inside the orthosis, electrodes deliver mild stimulation that help your hand move."*** The Bioness units cost $6000.00+. They offer payment plans.

*Tailwind.com

**Bioness.com

FIND A GOOD SUPPORT GROUP

19. They Get Another Piece of Me

I was home, safe and sound. Family around me, home cooked meals and sleep, sweet sleep. The wounds from the bleed outs were just about completely healed; there were just a few dressings to be changed once a day. Friends cooked dinners for my family and cared for Myles, giving him an escape from the drama at home. A couple of days a week, Myles was invited to spend the day at a buddy's house. My heart ached, when he'd come and sit on my bed, just to be near me. I so wanted to be a mother to him again.

My greatest challenge, at that point, was the constant pain. My toes that were as black as night and the top segment of my pinky finger on my left hand was pitch black. My arm, where one of the bleed-outs occurred, hurt when I lay down. I also could feel my right arm was slipping from the socket, no matter what we did, regardless of how we tried to support it.

The toes were slowly self-amputating, emphasis on the word "slowly." The Plastic surgeon wanted to "let nature to take its course." I wanted them to stop hurting. "Can we get this over with?" I'd ask him at each office visit. Four and a half months I suffered as they died and separated from my body. Four months, that's more than enough time to die, isn't it? So, finally, at one appointment with the Plastic surgeon, he agreed to remove the dead parts of my toes. He either got fed up with my ultimatums: "Take the toes off or shoot me!" or there was no need to wait any longer. I was so very tired of being in pain.

It was about five weeks after my stroke and the surgery was scheduled for early one morning. I was so very glad the plastic surgeon had agreed to not wait for the toes to fall off, and I was almost giddy on the way to the hospital that morning. I was given a general anesthesia for the procedure, probably because the doctor didn't want to hear,

"Are you done yet? Come on, step on it." After the surgery, I was brought up to a room where I was to spend the night, Michael was there waiting for me. The nurse got me settled in the bed and Michael asked to see my foot. The nurse uncovered my foot, removed the gauze and we simultaneously gasped at the sight of my foot having had two toes removed clean down to the base. The surgeon had removed all the phalange bones in number 3 and 4 toes. In the place where they had been, was a bloody hole.

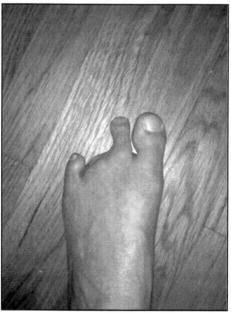

This is a good time to mention that my husband is a "flopper." When the man passes out, he flops. Michael was so sure they would just remove the tips of my toes. He was totally unprepared to see the hole on my foot where my, as he referred to them, "cute little toes" once resided. Within a minute, my "Rock of Gibraltar" was on the floor, flopping. The nurse panicked and called the EMT's to the floor to help him. I'd been here and done this before so, I knew the drill. He's out for maybe five minutes, flops for the first two to three minutes and then it's all quiet. In couple of minutes, he's back. I could just sat there and smiled. How terribly inappropriate, I know. I was learning that being "inappropriate" was going to be a big part of my life from here on out.

Back to my flopping husband. The EMT's came and took care of my husband, checking his vitals and so forth, When Michael had revived enough to walk, my oldest son had arrived and convinced him to go to his condo to rest. With some coaxing, he went.

I know that one way to block out something they don't want to hear is to put one's fingers in one's ears and repeat "Peanut butter, peanut butter." The only way I could block out what I SAW was, turn my eyes from looking at my toes and board the train that's destination is "DENIAL." All aboard!! I was not going look at them again until I got home. When nurses would change the dressing, I refused to look at my maimed foot.

When Michael left to go to my son's condo, all of a sudden I was completely alone. Now, it was my turn to panic. I could not talk and I was trying to get the nurse to bring Michael back, as he walked down the hall. I could say Michael's name, but my feelings of panic, rendered me speechless. Instead, she laughed at my plight. I was crushed that someone would see my inability to speak as humorous. Instead of being a comfort to me, she was mocking me and enjoying my situation. I shut down. Literally. I was convinced that no one gave a hoot about my well being. I just blocked out any one and everyone that came into my room for the next three hours. I never felt so vulnerable and unprotected my life. It was a terrible feeling. I cocooned myself from the world around me and just held tight till my husband returned. I fought to just breathe slowly and purposefully so as to keep control, repeating in my mind, "Michael is coming back, Michael is coming back..." over and over, like a mantra. Michael returned in three hours. I grabbed for him and hugged him, sobbing. There was no way I could communicate what had transpired between the nurse and me. This is the longest three hours I had ever lived through. When I relive this experience, just thinking about those terrible three hours, brings back such strong emotions. It brings a shudder up from my very core. I was confronting how much I had changed, especially emotionally. I had been a very strong and confident person before my stroke; it took a lot to rattle me. Now, every emotion seemed magnified, I felt weak and helpless, totally out of control and very vulnerable.

There is something that happens to the brain after a stroke. A survivor's personality can change. Emotions can be heightened or lessened. Me, my emotions were on "steroids." If something was just a little scary, in my newly minted brain, it was time to either shut down or RUN! An unkind response from my nurse had transformed her to "NURSEZILLA!" Her laughing at my situation, translated into a very personal threat. Normally, if someone treated me badly, I would have shrugged it off. Never was I one to hide or cower.

The flip side is just as powerful in that when something struck me as funny, I would laugh hysterically to the point that I couldn't breathe. This happened so often during church that I stopped going on Sunday morning altogether. The smallest thing would tip me over into uncontrollable laughing, so much so that I would have to lumber out of the back of the church. It was very disconcerting and embarrassing. In such a staid setting as the Anglican Church, it was very inappropriate to laugh, never mind laugh hysterically. If only I could find a Pentecostal Church, then it would just be seen as the "spirit of laughter" that had come over me.

20. Covert Operation

The tip of my finger was going through the throes of death, as had my toes. It would stab me with daggers of sharp pain all day and night. I was trying to take pain medication only at night, which would allow me to sleep with the pain at a dull roar. During the day I would try to cope by keeping occupied. There were days when I just had to get relief from the pain and I would in a "Percoset stupor" for hours. Every now and then, medication or no medication, a stab of piercing pain would jump the barrier of the drugs just to let me know who was boss. I was ready to say sad farewell to my pinky finger as I had once known it.

The date was set for the amputation, but not willingly by the surgeon. Once again my Doctor wanted to let the dead section come off naturally. Doctor, sir, babies are born NATURALLY, rivers flow to the sea NATURALLY. There is nothing NATURAL about a part of a finger falling off. Doctor B, one of the plastic surgeons,(a favorite of ours) was very candid with us, especially when I was dealing with my finger injury. He confided in us that the IV should have never been placed in my hand due to the fact that I had been diagnosed with vasculitis. The standard protocol for such was to enter through a vein in the groin. A larger vein is necessary to minimize the stress of the introduction of a needle and the medication.

The room in which the surgery was performed was not your typical operating suite. It looked like it could be a room where people dealing in black market items would meet to close the transaction. Maybe there was no "room in the inn" for my surgery, or maybe all the first class rooms were being used that day. What was supposed be a simple amputation, seemed to have turned into a "covert operation" that should be kept "under wraps" in the basement. It was a small, dark room with just few odd pieces of furniture and storage boxes. There wasn't even a nurse present. The surgeon scrubbed and prepped the hand himself. "What is this, the 18th century?" I ask my husband.

The physician administered an injection of some form of Novocain into my hand, at the base of the pinky. As he did so, he warned me that this type of pain medication was the most effective form that he could use (in the basement) and that this MIGHT be painful. "This is the 18th century!" "Where's the good stuff they used for power washing my rear," I thought to myself. It was as though I had *asked* for this and this is what I got for pushing ol' Mother Nature (The wench). I don't mean to give the impression that he was enjoying any of this, but he was just so matter of fact about the pain I might feel. I suppose I could be matter of fact about someone else's pain, given the chance. I had doctored plenty of gruesome, painful wounds having six adventurous sons; I didn't go to flopping, but I felt their pain and would do anything I could to alleviate it. (Although now, truth be told, I would most likely be laughing the whole time.)

He reached in the tray of tools on the stand and picked up a pair of "nippers" the kind I would use on the FARM to CUT WIRE when we put up a fence or did repairs. I thought, "Oh, Lord, this is not going to be good. Aren't wire nippers over-kill?" I remember doing a double take thinking surely he meant to grab that tiny, "cute" little scalpel.

My finger was either made out of pretty tough stuff or his "nippers" were as dull as a butter knife. He had to lean into the finger with the nippers to get the dead part separated from the live part. He worked and worked, grunting and groaning as he employed every bit of strength. I thought that for his finale, he was going to climb up on the table to get some leverage, finishing with beating his chest, having won the battle over my finger. All I have to say is that, whatever I was paying for that pain medication, it was way too much. When it came to it dulling the pain, IT DID NOTHING. When all was finished, I was convulsing, in tears, in my husband arms.

With the fingertip gone, the pain diminished in a couple of weeks and the wound healed over quickly. It healed much faster than the hole, where two toes were now absent. That had taken seven to eight weeks to close. Five years after losing my two toes, the site is still very sensitive to the touch. If I am on my feet for more than an hour, I

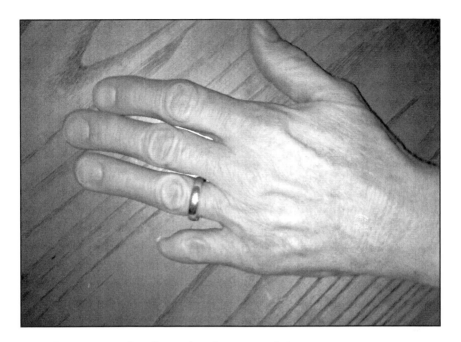

experience cramping from the three remaining toes over-compensating. If I catch it right away, I can back it down from a vise grip like cramp. If it goes past a certain point, I am in for 30 minutes of blinding pain. Waves of painful cramps come and go as it calms down and relaxes completely.

All we wanted now was to put some serious distance between what was left of my body and the hospital. I had a few follow-up appointments to track the healing of my toe. I missed the last one, because it was healing beautifully, and I was loath to go to the doctors office again. Not to mention we were out of money from paying for all these procedures and office visits. Each trip to the Doctor was another $100+ that we didn't have. It felt like the hospital and my doctors were like lint from the dryer, sticking to everything. If I didn't get far enough away, I would never be free of them. I wanted to keep what was left of my battered body.

When I was able to write/spell again in April, I started to write a blog. I had kept a journal since age 16, thanks to a high school teacher. I chronicled my life's events, every thing from new jobs, the move from New York to Massachusetts, meeting my husband, to the birth of my children. I wanted to record the impressions and feelings during my recovery. The victories, the frustrations, the people who saw me through, were all important to remember. I didn't realize then that my memory was going to need the "journal" in order to recall much of my journey. I thank God that the tendency that I had to chronicle events, feelings, etc., survived the stroke. So much of this recovery period would have remained a blur if not for my blog. One entry can ignite a whole stream of memories, some terribly painful, others funny. I did not want it to be an exercise in frustration. Writing with a pen was so difficult left-handed. Not to mention, I would probably not be able to decipher my handwriting. So, I typed on my laptop and recorded every significant event, emotional turmoil, etc. Thus, I entered the world of "blogging." This was my first entry almost five months after my stroke. Thank God for spell check!

http://hismercies.blogspot.com/2008_04_01_archive.html

Betrayal
Saturday, April 12, 2008

My body has served me well these 50 years, so I should be thankful, I am. I have taken good care of her, went out of my way to do it right. I feel betrayed by my body, abandoned by it. Of course my body has not a mind of its own, she is not doing this on purpose. Feeling like I am walking through a bad dream, not being able to hear my Lord. He hasn't left me, this I am sure of, but I need to hear my Lord.

21. Student Driver

How many people would volunteer to have a student driver take them to work, a different, student driver every morning? How many people would agree to a novice, a student doctor driving a wire, with hook on the end of it, through your veins? I don't see any hands raised. If your answer to such a question or suggestion is "Hell, no!", then I suggest not going to a teaching hospital for anything more than, say, an ingrown toe nail. You and your loved ones are fair game at teaching hospitals that takes the phrase "medical practice" to a whole, other dimension.

It was February and I had been home for two months. Early one morning, we got a call from Doctor M. telling us of the "need" to remove the IVC filter they had put in my vein in November. She told us that it needed to be removed right away and that it MAY have been in there too long. The filter can eventually adhere to the vein and possibly cause problems in the future. Problems? Me?

The time was set for the procedure the next day. I was still sketchy in my ability to speak, but I could manage well enough. I was wheeled to a small room with a curtain, where I changed into a gown and waited. A very young, fresh-faced looking woman doctor came in to explain the procedure to Michael and myself. She proceeded to recite the fact sheet she had obviously memorized the night before her fledgling flight, through my veins. That should have been our cue to "exit stage right" but we didn't, because we didn't think that this youngster was going to perform the procedure. Silly me, OF COURSE she was. This is a TEACHING hospital and I was her "over-sized lab rat!"

They had probably trolled the hospital records looking for some poor sucker to PRACTICE on; someone who was due to have the procedure done. The abruptness of the call and scheduling supported my theory and coupled with our recent history at this hospital made me suspicious of everything they said or did. This young resident needed a "vein fishing expedition" for her next doctor's "Girl Scout" badge. What do you think? They forgot to read the chart about what conditions I had, dictating the protocol for EVERYTHING? They gave me Prednisone instead of TPA? But they remembered an obscure little wire basket in my vein.

We asked a number of questions to which she had textbook answers. She just reiterated the complications that could arise if we left it in. Thinking back on the conversation now, I think she was afraid we'd change our minds and back out. She was under the impression that we knew we had an option; we had no idea that there was an option.

I was awake through the whole procedure and everything was coached by an older physician talking her through every aspect, start to finish. As I lay there listening to her coach, and her responses to him, I knew I was a "lab rat" in danger. She had to stop several times to collect herself. I was thinking, "Take all the time you need, honey."

The tension in the room could be cut with a knife, (or a pair of sharp wire nippers.) The beginning of the procedure was painless, but that wasn't going to last long. All of a sudden, I felt a sharp, piercing pain. "RED ALERT!! Abort! Abort!" Every move she made, caused more pain. She was having trouble extracting the wire "basket." It had, indeed, embedded itself in my vein.

I was being transported to the hidden dungeon under the tree, in the film *Princess Bride*, Count Tyrone Rugen, who was experimenting with his favorite torture machine, was about to ask me, "I'm sure you've discovered my deep and abiding interest in pain." "Presently I'm writing the definitive work on the subject, so I want you to be totally honest with me on how the machine makes you feel?" (The same character who said "If you haven't got your health, then you haven't got anything.")

I could see the screen of the monitor that she was using to drive through my veins, and from what I could see, that basket was not going anywhere, hook or no hook. There was a real danger of tearing the vein, and after what seemed like an eternity, the physician who was coaching her told her to stop. I said very loudly "I second that motion," expressing the fact that I had had enough. I was fed up with with being the hospital's "guinea pig" for beginners and "doctor wannabe's." The old Barbie bubbled up to the surface. "Time to go home!" <u>Never to return</u> to this institution's hallowed halls of horror.

<u>Courage ?</u>

Wednesday April 30 2008

People keep telling me I am courageous. I have news for you. I didn't stand in line for this, nor did I decide to sign up to be a part of God's plan. I obviously didn't read the fine print if I did sign somewhere!! I would get off this train NOW if I could, but its not being presented to me as an option. If I could conjure up a little miracle I would, I want out!!! I think it says volumes that God had to allow something so radical, so seemingly cruel to get through to me! People, this is not a profile in courage.

22. Drowning in Bills

In August 1992, I was in labor with my son Sam, fully prepared to have my sixth child at home. I had been in labor for two days, and I was experiencing abnormal severe pain in my back, the labor was not progressing. So, I was transported to Speare Memorial hospital in Plymouth, New Hampshire. We found out that the baby was pressing heavily on the ureter, the tube that drains kidney into the bladder. This restriction was causing my kidney to rupture, which was the source of the pain. I am but 5' 3", and Sam proved a very large baby (9 pounds, six ounces. My other children were no more than 8 pounds, five ounces). The decision was made to deliver him by C-Section. As soon as the surgery was over the pain stopped. Six hours later, it returned with a vengeance. The surgeon was called in, and after a brief examination, he ordered an MRI. Upon seeing the results, it was plain to him what had happened. I had been so dilated from being labor so long, and I was losing a lot of blood during the surgery. He closed me up quickly, and accidentally snagged the ureter in the sutures. Now, it was not a baby restricting the ureter, it was sutures. Again, the kidney was unable to drain, and was rupturing. So it was back to the OR. The surgeon went in, released the ureter, and all was well.

Three weeks after the surgery, we received a bill charging us for two surgeries. The cost of the surgeries came to, $17,000.00. Upon receiving the bill, my husband called the surgeon immediately, and he was indignant – but not because of my husband's call. Doctor Brentwood had at the time of the second surgery included a note to the file that the second surgery was correcting a condition caused by the first, and there should be no fees charged. He must have called the billing department immediately, for within two days all charges for the second surgery, and

MRI, were backed out of the bill, reducing it to about $7,000.00. Reasonable people finding reasonable solutions. Twenty years later, in Virginia, there was no "reasoning" with this hospital.

Nearly every time we had a procedure done, it was due to a mistake that the hospital had made at an earlier date. We were getting charged for these excursions to the hospital and the bills just kept coming. Every month there was handful of new bills to pay. It got to the point that it was so stressful to get the mail that I stopped asking Myles to go to the box every day. We had paid for appointments as we went, until the money ran out and then maxed out our credit cards. Then, they sued us. Calls from collection agencies started, four to six times a day. That was a very difficult time in our household; so many points of stress were rearing their ugly little heads. Our application for discounted fees was denied out of hand by the hospital. When we asked for the reason, it was told us that because we owned a home, the hospital's policy was to charge according to their standard fee schedule. Michael's explanation that the bank owned far more of our home than we did fell upon deaf ears. He spent much of the following three years defending lawsuits from the hospital, and the past seven years paying off the $100,000.00 in credit card expenses that were racked up.

We decided to get the records from the hospital because we knew there were mistakes made. We hoped some of them would be documented. They were, but they didn't want us to see those pages.

Every time we asked for a COMPLETE set of records, there were always pages missing. Finally, after three tries, we received the full set of records by asking for just the missing pages. There were notes made by physicians or their assistants, stating plainly the how and why of each blunder. We decided to counter sue, mainly because we thought we were going to lose our farm.

If the hospital had admitted the wrongdoing, we gladly would have walked away and just tried to pick up the pieces of our shattered lives. They had our backs against the wall; there would be no walking away. We honestly just wanted to be left alone.

Michael offered them a settlement that was 40 percent of the bill. We would sell off some of the land that we owned to raise the cash. It was rejected immediately. Two weeks before the expiration of the statute of limitations for filing our medical malpractice suit, we met a gentleman who owned a gift/antique store in Williamsburg. We chatted for ten minutes or so while we completed the purchase of a small birthday gift for one of our boys. Just as we were leaving, he asked what happened to my leg, as I was walking with my cane. I could have kissed him. Is that all the obvious injury he detected? I really like this man. I told him I had suffered a stroke. He was shocked because I was so young, and he expressed how sorry he was. I assured him that I was sorry enough for the both of us. We told him it was a long story and attempted to brush the inquiry off, not wanting to take up so much of his time. Before we knew it, we were sitting outside his store at a picnic table sharing the whole drama, start to finish. Mr. D. was getting more upset by the minute. By the time we were done with our tale he was visibly shaken. And that was the "Cliffs Notes" version. At some point, he started to take notes. "That's odd," I thought, a complete stranger so intrigued by my story, enough TO TAKE NOTES!! When we were done, he asked us what we were going to do. Michael told of his having been a lawyer in New Hampshire, and we were going to counter sue. If nothing else, it hopefully would slow the hospital down from their rabid pursuit of money.

Then Mr. D. told us that he was a semi retired attorney, and that he would like to help in any way he could. He was not a personal injury lawyer, but he would help file the counter suit, to make sure it got in in time. So, just before the deadline for the filing as an answer to the hospital's suit against us, Mr. D. filed the counter suit. We asked for a jury trial, because anyone listening to my story would realize the validity of my case. The case is now stalled because of "technicalities." The hospital is claiming <u>Sovereign</u> <u>Immunity</u>, the so-called protected right to operate a business for profit and not be held accountable for any mistakes, even if the mistakes prove to be fatal. (Which would have been the case if my husband didn't speak up in the ER.) Sovereign Immunity? What "KINGDOM" is this?

<u>Crying and laughing</u>
Monday, April 14, 2008

You would not think it strange if someone said they laughed every day, so what? I can say that and so can most people. Well, I find myself crying every day. The smallest thing will tip me over the edge. Things like seeing my horse in the pasture, having a hard time PUTTING MY SOCKS ON one hand-ed, or Myles asking me a question that requires a huge lengthy explanation.

People tell me crying is "cleansing," that God is reaching in and pulling out what needs pulling out, that I should just yield to it. I have no choice. It's not a "thing" that I can "yield" to. It takes over and doesn't let me go till it's through with me, which is kind of disconcerting. I have also acquired a new "primal" kind of noise that goes with it...fun.... especially when I cry in a public place. That's rich. But I should give laughing its due. I now laugh so hard that I find it hard to breathe. That leads me to another disconcerting group of noises. It is a wonder Michael takes me anywhere. I have seen a lit-tle more control recently, much to my relief, and Michael's.

23. The Tapestry of My New Life

Within four months of the stroke, I was walking slowly with a walker at home. I stopped using the wheel chair around the house as soon as I was able to stand for more than five minutes. Using the wheelchair was holding me back, not to mention that the trim on the doorways was taking a real beating. My whole recovery M.O. was to push the envelope on everything. Sometimes this got me in a lot of trouble. I spent a lot of time picking myself up off the floor. One time, I fell, breaking the impact with my face. I still have a dent in my cheekbone to show for it. With my right arm/hand "on vacation," I could no longer catch myself when I fell. More times than not, my approach got me those little victories that added up to make significant milestones. My tendency toward athleticism was a definite catalyst and aided my progress. I knew this was going to be a lot of hard work; I didn't shy away from it. I really didn't think about it, I just did it. Of course, I'm going to push myself. Of course, I'm going walk. When I would get overwhelmed with frustration, I'd have a darn good cry, wipe the tears from my face and go at it again. The most important thing I gained when at the week in rehab, that they emphasized over and over, that recovery from a stroke was a race against time.

By the time I was seven months post-stroke, it dawned on me. "This is your life, Barb. Time to suck it up and deal with it." There was a period of grieving, which included anger, red-hot anger. I wasn't angry all the time, but it would just hit me, out of the blue. The position in which I found myself, I felt I had to take responsibility for most of it. It was a lot to process. I LET THEM do this to me. This would surface off and on the first two years, lessening as time went on and as God healed my heart. Surely, more than my body was "broken." My heart was broken, too. I had yet to work through why God had allowed this. I had to put away what used to be me, who I was, and learn how to live in the here and now. The surrender of every thing was rarely pretty, or graceful. One of the hardest aspects of this was learning to ask for help BEFORE frustration took over. There is a fine line between pushing yourself in order make progress and knowing when to say "uncle." Uncle was not in my vocabulary prior to my stroke.

Daddy's Favorite
Monday October 20th 2008

*About two years ago, just before this "thing" started, I had the nerve to say to God " I really want to be one of your **favorites** and I want to know you better" I didn't think about it much, although I repeated it a few times, especially the "favorite" part. So, just about a week ago I was thinking about Job,(he was one of Gods favorites) and God reminded me of the prayer I prayed..... What was I thinking????*

I remember my father, Don, I always felt like his favorite. He played with me when he got home from work, pushing me on the swing, or giving me a "horseback" ride on his back. Crawling on all fours, rearing up so I would cling to him for all I was worth. I loved it, I loved him. I really felt his love for me , that's what I wanted from my heavenly Father.

You may think, He's got a funny way of showing His love.... stay tuned....

The whole hospital experience had been the antithesis of the "health care" I was used to. All I can think is that each event or error, led to another one, and it was nearly impossible to get off the "train" while it was in motion. As the issues that made up this train wreck continued, I knew that most of them were over my head, way over. Like the one inch thick slab of my hip and buttocks, peeling off of my body. Nothing I had ever encountered would have given me the tools to cope effectively with this. I think back on the parasite issue and I regret not taking the veterinarian's advice and use the "worm medicine" that he gave his son, successfully bringing him back to health. Knowing the "old me," I'm still wondering why I didn't take his advice. It was as though I was another person altogether.

Something that I was missing sorely was being able to hear God. I knew that surely He had not left me, but I could no longer discern

His voice. It was as though my internal voice was blocked. I had trouble hearing myself think and had a very short attention span, not unlike a CB scanner. I'd have a thought and lose it in a split second. I was fully "blonde." I was no longer dreaming at night either. It was just a deep silence, not even a cricket. Now, that's bad. My family would tell me something and I'd forget what was said in a half an hour. Even now, friends share things with me, then they might add, "Don't say this to anyone." Their confidences are safe with me. I usually never think again about what they have shared. Into the black hole that has become my memory bank. It seems that what has nothing to do with me personally, just falls off into the abyss. Into the black hole it goes.

I would have a hard time gathering my thoughts to pray. People would come and pray with me and my mind would wander, sometimes looking at their feet, "Man those are huge feet," wondering what size shoes they were wearing. If my mind wandered into something funny that happened that day (like Myles's animation recounting an injury), I'd hold it as long as I could, then, like water bursting through a dam breach, I would "lose it," laughing. This was very embarrassing early on; I just wanted "normal me," back.

My speech was improving so much that I could talk on the phone with my Mom. I know where that saying "I want my Mommy" comes from. When you find yourself in a situation that draws you into a childlike helplessness, you want your Mom. It seemed a natural response. When I would call her, she would wait patiently wait for me to finish my sentences, never trying to fill in the gaps, of which there many. I would have to think of each word in my head before I said it. My mother was a real cheerleader and a constant source of information for me. She was continually cutting out articles she'd find while reading the newspaper or a medical magazine about new technology for stroke survivors. She shared my "Let's fix this" attitude. She came to help me with the upkeep of the house and the cooking. Driving all the way from Hamburg, New York, to our farm in Virginia, at age 85 by herself. Guess where I learned to "push the envelope?" Helen Sheff!

Our relationship began to grow and deepen. She was heartbroken to see me in this state. The little disagreements that we'd over the years seemed frivolous now. Instead, we'd reminisce and laugh, then reminisce and cry. It was such a healing balm to me. My sister, Pat, who was not working at the time, also came off-and-on to support the effort. She'd keep the house, laundry, kids and critters on track. My brother, Don, called many times during the week, to keep abreast of my progress. He has worked for 30+ years, as a Profusionist, running the heart-lung machine during open-heart surgery. He is very knowledgeable of the workings of hospitals. We were able to bounce issues off him. Later, as we poured through the hospital records, he would help bring clarity to what we were reading.

After a while, I was able to walk around the house, but my right arm was hanging useless at my side. I gained some ability to lift it and to bend it, but the use of my hand was not coming back. My arm would occasionally knock something over. It was very upsetting that I lost control of a part of me, as though it was no longer a part of my body. I can grip with my hand, but I have to engage every muscle in my body to do it, and if the fist is closed, I can't relax it voluntarily. "The 'claw' is going to get you," I laughingly said at times, when I would try and reach for my son, Myles.

I can no longer run, play guitar, sing, play soccer or baseball. However, now six years later, I can drive, garden, walk, talk, THINK, pray, and hear my Lord. After three years, I started to have dreams again. Just recently, I had a dream and in it, I was dreaming. A dream within a dream. That's real progress, wouldn't you say? I concentrate on what I CAN do, and am grateful for each thing that has been restored!

Just for the record, I am now helping Myles with math. By the time Algebra is required, (in the perfect world there would be no need for Algebra), I will have him tutored like his older brothers.

One of the books I bought from Amazon was an account of a person who had a massive left-brain stroke at a young age. This professional shared their experience that seemed so foreign to all the other stroke survivor's stories. They described a journey into tranquility and peace, coupled with euphoria!! This person had a complete recovery. "I have to talk to this person" I said to myself. So I wrote and eagerly hoped and waited for a reply. The letter that came back in reply was not what I expected. I was told to "stop wallowing in self pity and just work at recovery everyday".

The letter I had written was short, and described my stroke, briefly. I read mine to my husband and then read to him, the letter I received back from this stroke survivor. I asked him what his take on it was. He was dumbfounded. "Maybe it was just a bad day they were having," he said. That put the brakes on my applying to anyone else for "input."

Just Humming Along...
Friday July 25th 2008

There I was just humming along, for the most part minding my own business, and BAM!!!! Life changes in a second, one minute your walking and talking, the next day you can't do either. How can I explain it, how can I make you, the reader, all three of you, see what this is like. I used to throw a ball from third base like a rocket, now I can't even move my fingers!! This is a cruel joke someone played on me. God???

Do I sound like I am complaining ? Maybe I am....I want you to understand how fast life can change, AND what this has done to change my life. Well, first, I have a new mission in life, I want to talk with people who have had strokes! I want to, with Gods help, reach into that lonely, broken place, and pull as many people out of that "hell" as I can. I want to be there to cheer them on, pick them up when they need it, and listen to them cry or laugh, usually at inappropriate times, and do it with them!!!! Try and show them what a LOT of hard work will do, and show them its worth it in order to get your life back. To push the limits of everything! Try everything! How my life has changed.....

*I made dinner now twice. First time I needed help with opening the cans for tuna pasta salad, but next time I made the meatloaf all alone. I cook pancakes, sometimes **with** egg shells for added fiber. I have ventured into grilled cheese some. This has been a real personal victory, for someone who likes to cook, I want everyone to revel in it with me. I ask everyone to take a moment at the meal before we start, to revel in my accomplishment.*

I am venturing to talk on the phone now. How life has changed. I have dreaded talking on the phone!!!

I can shower alone, not Michael MINDED, not all, but for my sake he is glad to see me graduate.

I am only on two medications now and they will be done to one in a couple of weeks. I can walk in the driveway now!!! The rocks used to throw me off balance. I am able to do the laundry now, I've been at it for a couple of months. I am not in so much pain now. A hundred more things have changed since the stroke, things I now can do and things I can't do YET, the next big hurdle is driving, this has been one of the hardest things , I hate being trapped...... stay tuned that's gonna soon change!

A stroke is a life-changing event for anyone. The world as you know it is gone, sometimes for good. It's natural to seek advice from those who have traveled that road. I wanted to glean whatever tidbit of information I could, knowing that there was a full recovery. I wanted to know how that happened. It seems that every stroke leaves its mark, sometimes it is easily erased, other times not. Having my body dictate limitations was a very foreign concept to me, I had been the master and my body was always willing to go where I asked it to go. I have not stopped asking my body to perform things that are seemingly impossible. I will always continue to try and squeeze what I can out of "her," but not to incite anger and debilitating disappointment. I have learned to guard my heart from emotions that deny or try and discard gratitude for what I have has been restored to me. I like to recite those things that I can do out loud, just to cement the feelings of gratitude. I know others who have not regained what I have. That is big fat dose of reality that helps, to keep my life in a proper perspective.

24. Driving Miss Barbie

About nine months after the stroke, I wanted to drive my car again. To be able to run simple errands like grocery shopping, taking Sam to Community College, etc. Michael had been taking me to the store to shop since I was back in the kitchen cooking again. I hated being chauffeured. I wanted normal back in my life. Usually DMV takes your license away when you have a stroke. For some reason that didn't happen. I was somehow was flying under the radar. Maybe they were expecting me to relinquish it. (Fat chance) Ignorance is definitely bliss.

At seven months post-stroke, foolishly, I wanted to try to drive my car again. My right leg was unable to operate the gas pedal. To apply just the right amount of pressure and to be able to quickly release the pedal, was an impossible task to ask my leg to do. I was so disappointed, I cried as I got out of my car.

Two months later, I was ready to try again. This time I was determined to make it over this hurdle. Michael got in the car, and I got in the driver's seat. I was going to do this "by hook or by crook." Whatever body parts I would have to employ, I'm going to drive!! I had recently heard of a person who had had a stroke, who was now driving with only the left foot. So, I tucked my right foot in, and used my left foot to operate the gas and brake pedal. I practiced while sitting in the driveway. It was a little strange at first, but it worked. I drove slowly around our country block, about three miles, savoring every moment. Of course, tears were streaming down my face, tears of joy! I was free! I have to say that at seven months post-stroke, "I foolishly" want to drive again, I realize now that I was far from mentally ready. When I started driving at nine months, even then, I was not ready. God is merciful, and I never had an accident. For the first couple of months I never went far. I waited before driving on major highways where speed was a necessity.

Taking the Offensive!
Sunday, July 12, 2009

Maybe its because I was a rebellious child growing up, that this come naturally. Now that I'm on the right side of the law, so to speak, this "rebellion" still comes in handy, but it displays itself in constructive ways. I'm not crawling out windows at midnight anymore. Now, it is more like taking the offensive against anything and everything that stands in the way of a goal. Following God more closely or doing something when my body says, "No, you can't do that!" "Oh, yeah? Watch me!"

Michael and I were going out to dinner, as we have done every Friday night. I was meeting him in town. There was no parking near his office so I had to park a long way from the building. I called Michael and he said he'd be there in "five." SUUURRRE." I had heard THAT before. There was a "pot holed" parking lot, a street with a big curb, and small hill to maneuver. Imagine these being my "obstacles!" Everything is oh, so relative. I was so mad that something as mundane as a curb, pot holes, and a hill would prevent my going in to the office on my own. I said to myself, "I can do this." Fifteen minutes later, I did, by God's grace.

Now that I was mobile, I could go shop by myself. I never really minded shopping before the stroke, but now the new me had to steel myself every time I went. I had gone from an athletic, confident, outgoing woman to walking in a state of humiliation constantly, especially in the early stages of recovery. When my right hand was not tucked into my pocket, it was swinging like a metronome, keeping the cadence of my walking stride. When people see you're disabled they treat you very differently, everything from condescension, to pointing and laughing, to outright rudeness. You are now seen as less than a whole person.

I was shocked at this phenomenon. I was now walking in other people's shoes, tasting a slice of life that I had at one time only observed from a distance. It was incredibly painful; I cried rivers of tears that first couple of years because in my mind, I was less than a whole person. It took me a while to shed that estimation of myself, and it would have been much harder if I didn't know God. All the "positive thinking" or "Build Your Self Esteem" CDs could not bring me through to the other side of this mountain! All that I could see was the physical evidence that cemented that feeling of inadequacy. Now I have come to the realization, that I am "changed" more than "broken." The term broken, focuses attention on the losses that I have suffered. I am moving past that image of myself. I have been changed in many ways, because of what I have gone through, but I refuse to get stuck in broken.

I went back to reading the Bible daily, as was my habit prior to my stroke. The scripture that really helped me was Colossians 3:2 — "Set your mind on things above, not on things on the earth." It is a reminder that if your hopes are stuck in this ol' dying world, that is passing away, you are bound to be miserable.

Because I had trouble reading for any length of time, I would listen to the bible on CDs. Good old Alexander Scourby was gently feeding my spirit the truth about who and what I was — a child of the living God. It was coming back to me!! Scriptures that I had memorized as a young Christian began to resurface in my memory. It was a very powerful and profound journey.

Reckless Abandon!!
Wednesday, April 28, 2010

Since the stroke, I have feared many things, as small a thing as falling or something big like stroking again. Job said, "FOR THE THING I HAVE FEARED HAS COME UPON ME, WHAT I HAVE DREADED HAS HAPPENED TO ME." (Job 3:25) I need to exercise the muscle called FAITH. It must be tested, proven, refined! If what God gave us through His Son is truly incorruptible, then we have nothing to fear! Even when bad things happen, God can bring beauty from ashes.

I'm really not sure when I realized my fears were based on satan 's (small "s" purposefully) lies and his whispers as my brain came back "on line." I had lost so much of my cognitive ability – spelling, math, (Okay there wasn't a lot to lose there) the ability to read... I remembered my faith and what it was based on, THE HOLY WRITTEN WORD OF GOD!! So I had CDs of the Bible and until I could read well again I listened to them. What a joy to hear Mr. Scourby speak the Word of God. Sometimes I would just start the CD and start to cry. "I'm coming back, Lord," I would say in my mind because I couldn't speak very well. NOW I know, what I knew before, satan is liar!

Lately God has been speaking to me about the in-dwelling Christ, God in us, His fullness is in Christ and Christ is in me. That's what the Word says. That's huge. God makes His home in those that believe. That's why "Church" happens whenever two or more gather. Exceedingly, abundantly more than we ask or THINK, according to the power that works in us! Now. If that doesn't incite reckless abandon, nothing will. According to the eternal purposes which He accomplished in Christ Jesus our Lord, in whom we have BOLDNESS and access WITH CONFIDENCE through FAITH IN HIM!!! Spirit of Worship rises up in me...

25. What's for Dinner?

I began to cook about five or six months after my stroke, something that I really had missed doing. I didn't realize HOW MUCH I missed it until I starting poking around in the kitchen again. One day it came to me like a lightening bolt....Standing in the middle of the kitchen I declared, "I love cooking!" From the time I was a young girl, it was a joy to feed family and friends. I am no gourmet cook, but no one has taken ill or died from my cooking either, so I'm somewhere in between.

I was doing it now one-handed, so there were some adjustments needed in my approach. Instead of having to ask someone to open a can, I bought special can opener. I learned to use alternative parts of my body for opening, mixing, closing, etc. I would put a blanket below where I was sitting, place a bowl that contained something that need-ed light mixing, between my knees, and commence stirring. The blan-ket was to offer the bowel a soft landing if it slipped out of my grasp. Same for opening jars. I'd use the "death grip" of my knees. It rarely fails. You can only begin to imagine how I used my teeth. I can open just about anything with my teeth. Classy, eh? Spreading cream cheese on a bagel, or buttering a piece of toast? Put the toaster on a towel to weigh it down, lay the bread on the towel, and you have a stable place for the bread while you spread the butter. To slice open a bulky roll, I use scissors. I back it against the refrigerator that is right next the counter, and I work the scissors in until it is opened all the way around.

Whenever I was going to use my heavy enameled cookware for casseroles, I would assemble all the ingredients with the dish sitting on the oven rack in the oven. So dishes that were just too heavy or too risky to try and place it in the oven one-handed, would be already in the stove.

I could slide the pans full of water along the counter, the sink being a small piece of counter top away from the stove. We replaced the gas stove, because there was no way, single-handed, to keep the frying pan from slipping around on the raised burner grates. Little by little, I figured out how to do what I love doing in the kitchen, one-handed. I was back in the saddle in my kitchen!

I started with simple things and worked my way up to the more difficult. I remember the first dinner I made. I was so very happy to be cooking something, even something as basic as a meatloaf. I wanted to take a minute after prayer, to have the family just look at what I had accomplished. What a milestone for me. It was exhausting. At that time, I was still sleeping a lot, two naps a day. Jokingly, I asked for a moment of reflection in honor of my great feat, before they dug in, "Sorry mom, I'm hungry." "Well then, how about a photo op?" That fell on deaf ears. They had been eating what my husband called cooking, and to be kind, that's not one of his gifts. How long can growing boys live on spaghetti, hot dog and beans?

Sipping the Cup....
Monday, December 15, 2008

Jesus said, "If it be your will take this cup away from me; nevertheless not My will, but yours be done." Well, He drank the whole cup. That was God's will. He confirmed it again, in His statement, "Permit this." When one of His disciples cut the ear off of one who was arresting Him, no one took note as Jesus reached out and healed the man's ear. Were they focused or what? Rabid, I call it.

"He who abides in Him ought to himself also to walk just as He walked." 1 John 1:6

God asks us to sometimes drink from the cup of suffering, to share in Christ's lot. "Me. Pick me," we say, right? Not quite. Maybe if I keep a low profile. You know, not make waves, and He'll pass me by. OR maybe if I pray everyday, GO TO CHURCH, tithe, 15 percent, that'll keep Him off my scent. It's funny that when we want something from God, we do the same things. GOING TO CHURCH, tithe, pray. Hmmmmm?

Well lately I feel like I've sipped from the "cup." Not a big drink compared to Christ, but a sip.

I thought it would bear fruit. It should right? Still, I find myself getting really angry at the different situations in which I find myself in. God's put a lot of things in my lap that would humble most people. Being stripped of everything should make one appreciate the things that are given back. Not me. It just has made me want more! Ingrate! True confessions, if I were Jesus standing next to the guy with the ear that just got lopped off, I wonder if I would have laid my hands on him to heal him. When I look around, or hear of others' trials, that's enough to bring me to my knees in repentance. I've really felt this the last three weeks or so. In the past, I could just take a deep breath when my "sleeping" arm knocked something over, or when I couldn't open a jar with my usual tricks. Why now? When I have come so far, why should I lose hope? Lose patience. Maybe this is just a phase. What triggers these phases? I've found myself crying a lot. Today, I went out to see my horse and I unexpectedly started wailing. Good thing I was alone! Maybe it's more grieving, I thought that was over and done with....

26. Forgiveness and Freedom

The entry above was written in my blog, one year after my stroke. I had not forgiven any of the players that were involved in my case. This anger and frustration was simmering just below the surface, so every roadblock, every bump in the road scratched that surface. I was continually, in my subconscious, blaming the hospital for the wreck my life had become. I have since forgiven the hospital, the doctors, nurses and aides, who made mistakes and/or treated me badly. That has been very freeing and healing.

What tipped me off that this was an unresolved issue was that at about three years post-stroke, whenever I heard a TV or radio commercial for the hospital, going on about how wonderful they were, I'd turn it off. Walking over to the radio saying to myself, " Yeah, yeah, blah, blah, blah." Then one day the Lord said to me, "Wouldn't just be easier to forgive the hospital and staff than have to interrupt what you are doing to turn the radio off?" It was as though He were appealing to the practical, efficient side of my personality. I laughed at first, but then realized how serious this was. I was in a prison of my own making. I was playing right into satan's hands or "ugly" as I refer to him. I forgave everyone. So I went down the list, from every doctor, nurse, aide, the hospital, and the rehab. I had to forgive each and everyone who played a part. Some of the people it took three and fours rounds, over a few months, to nail it down. Some, I had to take a hard line and pray for them. Try and hold unforgiveness in your heart while you are praying a blessing over someone. It can't be done.

Today as I sat to down write, there was a "news flash" on the radio. It was the top story of the day in the city where the hospital is located. I found the news article in the local online newspaper:

"Nearly 30,000 patients are admitted to the _____ _____ Medical Center each year, **but many of those patients may be leaving the hospital in worse shape than they arrived.** According to the _____ Hospital Safety Score, the ____ Med Center received a "D" grade in terms of preventable accidents, doctor error, and medical mistakes between 2009 and 2011." In the area _of death_ from complications after surgery, _____ scored 135.77, more than twice as high as the best performing hospital score of 54.9.

Of course this was not news to me. I was their darned "poster child." After the hospital sued us for about $200,000 for the "care" they had given me, I, with the help of my husband, and the Medical Safety Consultant wrote a letter to the president of the hospital and the Board of Visitors, and copied it to the CEO of the hospital. The Medical Safety Consultant spent hours pouring over the records, and was able to clearly identify the mistakes that were made. So with her report in hand, I explained why we were counter suing. I described in detail the injuries I had suffered at the hands of the hospital and its employees and affiliate physicians. The response was a collective yawn and then the proverbial "buddy pass" to their attorneys. This is a state entity, and is protected by an antiquated rule called Sovereign Immunity. In other words, they believe they are IMMUNE from any claims for negligence. What incentive does the hospital have for excellence when they consider themselves immune to consequences? Obviously none.

27. Making Deals with God

When I was nineteen years old, I found myself in real trouble. Living on my own in Jamestown New York, I worked at a local restaurant and through my contacts there I became acquainted with some shady characters who were, dealing drugs. I had tried marijuana in my college years, but was never interested in doing anything more potent. A friend told me about a job opportunity and that I should meet with this person to see if it was something I would like to do. I went to the man's house and he explained the opportunity to me. The job was, smuggling cocaine out of South America into New York City in tuna cans! No experience required. No brains either! He promised me that I would be "set for life" from the money I would make. I was a single woman who, had no family that would miss me if I got caught and was rotting in a prison in South America. I was the perfect fit for the job!

I said "NO!" Even though the answer was no, I was followed by a couple of federal agents, who were after this man for his drug related activities. They were not very subtle or discreet, "Barney Fife" and his sidekick, followed me daily. I got so bold as to wave to them one day. Then one day it just hit me, "Is this where my life is going, getting invited to smuggle drugs for the promise of riches?" I knew there was a God, I'd been raised Catholic, but I had no idea how to get to Him. The long hard look at my life told me I was on the wrong track heading for the wrong destination. So I purposed to clean up my act on my own. I could not do it. No matter what kind of resolve or effort I poured into changing my ways, I failed miserably. I read books, calling on the teachings of Ram Dass the "guru" for happy living and having a peaceful heart. I tried Transcendental Meditation, Yoga, and many more. I felt they all were empty and lame.

Then my mom asked me to go with her on vacation to South Carolina for two weeks. She was driving a car that was questionable in its ability to get her and my sister to their destination. I was invited for my mechanical abilities. We were not in a great place in our relationship at this point in time. I had left home at seventeen and didn't look back. I was a rebellious child, especially after the death of my dad. My mom had to go to work as a nurse and it was stressful raising three teenagers alone. It was a house full of wounded people.

I was in between jobs, having left a job at a restaurant. This sounded like a good way to break away from "Barney Fife" and his partner. As I prepared for the trip, it was as though a dark cloud overshadowed me. I became fearful about going. I felt that this was going to lead my death and that I was not coming back. I had several dreams that woke me at night, dreams about the same truck hitting us head on. It was too late. I could not back out on my commitment to go now.

So I got on my knees and "brokered" my first deal with God. I said to the CREATOR OF THE UNIVERSE, (the nerve right?) "If You bring me back alive from this trip, I will serve You all the days of my life." Short and sweet. No haggling, no counter offers; just a bold faced proposal. He had me right where He wanted me.

On our trip to South Carolina we had only one problem. My mother was turning around after making a wrong turn late on the first day of travel, and she jackknifed the camper trailer we were pulling. She pinched and cut the wires between the bumper and the trailer that controlled the lights and the brakes. I was able to shorten the wires and rewire the plug and we were on our way. Wiring 101 at Alfred State had paid off. That was the only real issue that arose. We had a great time. There was healing in my mom's and my relationship. I was somehow changed. Little did I know that God had started my new life at the point I made the deal. HE knew I was coming back.

When we got back two weeks later, my mom dropped me off in Jamestown, and we said our goodbyes. I got down on my knees, on the walkway to my old Victorian house, and kissed the ground. Then looking heavenwards said to God, "I'm yours." Keeping my end of the deal. I moved home for three months and allowed God time to bring healing and restoration to my relationship with my Mother. Then, I moved to Massachusetts where I knew no one, but a man had hired me to start an equestrian school. I spent a lot of my days alone and God used that time to grow me up in my faith.

As the physical cost of my stroke played out, I began to take a good look at what was left of my world. There was some real heartbreak that faced me every day. The athleticism to which I was accustomed was now reduced to simply picking myself up off the floor without needing help. I was accustomed to playing my guitar and singing to the Lord, writing some 30+ songs to Him over the years. Singing was a big part of my and my life, and it was now gone. People say, "Oh, everyone can sing." Well I can't, not even badly. The vocal chords won't allow this kind of exertion. Nothing distinguishable comes out. I "talk" through a song, but to say the words quickly requires great concentration. I'm not giving up. I still practice when I am alone. I wear my headphones with my favorite songs cranked up, and I "croon" away. On the upside, it keeps the mice at bay.

Another painful loss was that of relationships, people I considered friends. I found that when the rubber met the road, some friends were nowhere to be found. After the initial help with dinners, very few kept in contact with me. Let's face it – I could not "do" much anymore. Invitations stopped. Seldom did people visit me. I felt useless and hurt. Loneliness is a very real consequence of stroke. After the initial outpouring of aid, there may come a sickening silence. My life was so very full. Engaged in a plethora of activities, I was rarely alone. I never minded being alone before my stroke. Anyone who has raised children knows that alone-time is a welcome thing. This WAS NOT ALONE-TIME. This was, "You ARE ALONE, because you have nothing to offer," time. A few people did come to visit me, but when you life is going 70 MPH, and then suddenly comes to a screeching halt, there is bound to an adjustment period, a vacuum. I fought loneliness much of that first year. My inner drive to rehabilitate my body was, many times, the thing that would pull me out of the "vacuum" that enveloped me. So one Saturday in April, I found myself making another "deal" with God.

A Deal With God
Saturday, April 18, 2009

Every now and then reality gangs up on me and hits me square in the face. Usually by this time of the year my gardens are well underway. Not this year. Oh, I still have plans but I'm relying on others to make it happen, I HATE THAT !!!! You're breaking my heart, Papa....

So I will make a deal with You God. Give me the measure of the spirit, YOUR SPIRIT, the measure you have allowed "ugly" to take from me in the flesh. I will be satisfied.

Give me in the Spirit the measure of your Spirit to replace the "friends" that have gone away and I will rest in that. Give me in the Spirit, the measure that I sorely miss in singing praise and I will be full.... Give me in the Spirit the full measure of the strength that was mine. Remember: I WAS STRONG!! OK? OR you can restore all these things that were mine before, but only if I can keep the measure of Your Spirit. The full measure of our deal. Does this work for you? Sign right here_____. OR just say "Yes" That's good enough for me.

I love you Lord, my Papa.

This "deal" helped me identify and name the hurts and losses that I was having trouble accepting. It put me in a place where I relinquished these and I felt this was something that God was waiting for. Even though that surrender has had to come in phases, this was definite beginning. I was not walking away from them with nothing tangible in return for my surrendering to Him. It is true when we are willing to let go of things in the natural we can receive more in the spirit realm. Putting away things of the flesh, for more of the Spirit. I've learned that God WANTS us to expect from Him. What child doesn't expect from their father? As I let go, and as I began to pray for those friends who had hurt me, I found forgiveness. There was a peace and undeniable joy. This process of surrender was going to take years, but it was a milestone for me to confront my losses head on. The scripture that I have repeatedly gone back to is Colossians 3:2 – "Set your mind on things above, and not on things on the earth." If I could discipline myself to keep my eyes, thoughts, and heart on the Spiritual realm, and not be held in the grip of the "things" of the world, there would be no stopping me! Like the apostle Peter; he was walking on the water and he sank, because he looked at his CIRCUMSTANCES!

28. Just Say "No" to Velcro

"Velcro is for old ladies, and you are 39, right?" I used laugh with my Mother, that her sneakers were fastened with Velcro straps. She'd chuckle and say she was just "getting lazy in her old age." Truth be told, it was her arthritic fingers that made tying shoes an exercise in frustration. When I was back to walking, I really did not pay attention to how I was making that happen. I paid little mind to the Velcro straps on my shoes. "What else is a one-handed person to do?" It seemed *a given* at the time. As I became more and more aware of myself, I realized one day, "I'm not an old lady, I'm not doing Velcro anymore!" I decided to learn to tie my shoes with one hand and my teeth. I had spoken with a friend whose sister had a stroke at very young age, and she had learned to tie her shoes with her teeth. That's all I needed to hear. In one hour, I had it mastered. Shoes tied tight and secure. This was a bit of the normalcy I craved. Although tying shoes with my teeth could hardly be considered normal.

I was back in the pool the first summer after my stroke. It was the exercise I longed for to bring back some of my former strength. It took me all summer to gain back the lung capacity to keep my head under water for the whole length of the pool. We bought the pool with my Real Estate earnings, when most the boys were still at home. It was the hub of family gatherings during the summer. It was a huge oval that was 18'x 40.' It was very easy to do laps – especially in a circular motion. Being one handed, swimming in circles came naturally. I don't call it swimming exactly, but "flailing" with style.

Gardening was the next piece of my life I was looking to restore. It wasn't hard to get down on the ground to work in the dirt. To get up before the sun set, that was the hard part. We designed raised beds off the deck. I already had flowers growing in beds. Being a practical person, I decided to concentrate more on what we could eat, not what smelled good. By the time we left the farm, if planned well, there were sufficient plots to raise enough food for a family of four. I canned tomatoes that had I grown last summer, something that I had done before my stroke and wanted to prove to myself, that I could still do it. I think I should write the a book called *One-Handed Cooking and Canning for Dummies.*"

Pruning
Tuesday, October 21, 2008

"Every branch that bears fruit He prunes, that it may bear more fruit"
"Therefore do not cast away your confidence, which has great reward. For you have need of endurance so that after you have done the will of God, you may receive the promise."(Hebrews 10:35-36) As I read Job and what he endured, listening to all his complaints, he questioned God's care and love for him. That's only natural. The poor guy! After all, he was minding his own business and BAM!!! Sounds familiar to me. God was interested in making a good guy even better. He was obviously one of God's favorites. Remember God said to the snake, "What about my servant Job, he's quite a guy eh?" paraphrased a little bit. God was about to allow the enemy access to Job. "Only spare his life." Thanks. That's comforting. God knew the end from the beginning. He knew Job was going to go, maybe kicking and screaming, to another level of understanding of God. He was going get pruned (like it or not) so that he could bear more fruit. So it really backfired on ol' satan.

So, I see now it's not about our comfort, but it's about being made into the image and likeness of God.

29. Clots Strike Again

Late one evening in December 2010, I was experiencing a lot of pain in my back where the kidneys are located. I went to bed to try and get some sleep but the pain kept me wide awake. At dawn, I was up pacing the floor trying to decide what I should do. I had kept in touch with Dr. A and his wife after my stroke so I decided to call him.

He suggested I go to the ER at a different local hospital. So Michael drove into the city, in a blinding snowstorm. It was so bad that were passing many disabled vehicles along the way. My Kia Sportage with four-wheel drive, one of the best investments we ever made, was just blowing past the cars along the side of the road. Michael was as "cool as a cucumber," dodging and weaving to miss all the stranded vehicles. By the time we arrived I was in misery. My husband and I were greeted in the ER by a woman who, seeing the discomfort I was in, had me doing intake right away. After some tests were done, it was discovered I had a clot in my left kidney. There was some debate as to where the clot came from but the urologist said we would have to drain my kidney manually. "Manually?" "How do you drain a kidney manually?" I asked, afraid to hear the reply. He began to explain that if the kidney has a clot lodged in the ureter, as mine had, draining it manually was the only way to relieve the pressure and assure proper function. To accomplish this, a small tube is inserted through the skin and into the kidney. With one end of the tube in the kidney, the other end can then be attached to a collection bag outside the body and the urine can drain into it. "A collection bag?" "So let me get this straight, I now have to empty my kidney through a hose attached to a bag that I wear 24/7?" "That's correct." I felt like I was back in that dark little room ready to have my fingertip lopped off, and was being told that the pain meds probably would not work. Very matter of fact, as though EVERYONE has a bag to drain their urine! I half expected to hear him say, "Do you have a problem with that?" Do doctors take a required course in medical school called "Indifference 101?" So, without further ado, the doctor poked a hole just below my last rib, and inserted the tube it into my kidney. Then connected the other end of said hose to a bag. He then showed me how to empty "my bag" when it was full. I went home fitted with my brand new "plumbing" and collection bag. "How old am I? 85?" I asked my husband on the way home. I felt like I was entering a whole new realm, one I was going be in for the next 8+ weeks until my kidney revived enough to do its own dirty work. "Well that takes care my social calendar for the next two months," I thought on way home.

As though wearing this bag toting my urine was not bad enough, the entry site was very painful. Ah, yes, my old nemesis, pain. This time, it only hurt when I laughed or lay down. Pain and I were, it seemed to me, constant and inseparable companions. I stopped asking God "Why?" I began to ask "What?" What are you teaching me? I have to say that in my prayer times, the reoccurring message was, "Trust Me." Abraham was instructed to kill his only true son, to lay him on the altar and put to death, literally and figuratively, all his hopes and dreams. He didn't question God. He just did it. God stopped Abraham just before he struck the blow. Learning to rest, to trust in the midst of a storm, will allow us to be able to "walk on the waters" of life, regardless of the wind and the waves. Not judging God's love and care by the naked eye. Not bowing the knee to anything, fears, pain, feelings etc. I went in and out of this lesson several times in the last few years.

As the weeks passed and the pain at the entry point of the tube continued, I began to notice that less and less urine was draining into the bag. Despite the amount of fluids I drank, it was just a trickle of my "tinkle" that was being collected. After several trips back to the urologist to see if the tube was infected or misplaced, he told me, "It normally should not cause you this much pain." It was decided that my kidney had died. The kidney was going to shrivel up like a prune, so the doctor told me. "This happens a lot to me, the 'shriveling up like a prune' thing. First my toes, then my finger, and now a kidney!"

I thought to myself. The doctor removed the drain hose, leaving behind a hole in my side that oozed for months. So, I am minus one kidney now. I remind myself that a LOT of people have one kidney "missing in action." That's somewhat of a comfort to me. Somewhat.

Looking Through the Wounds
Monday, June 7, 2010

"Looking thru the glass darkly, but then face to face. Now I know in part, but then I shall know just as I am known." 1 Cor 13:12

To be carnally minded is death, but to be spiritually minded is life and peace." Romans 8:6

When life chews you up and spits you out, when wounds of sorrow pierce to your very core, its next to impossible to see clearly with your naked eyes.

Looking around me, looking at my life, I see a train wreck. Oh, there were survivors. No physical deaths. But I feel like I died just the same. Left with the pieces of a shattered life, that once was full of possibilities, I am FORCED to my knees, to plead with the Father, lover of my soul, to show me what is the reason for my life now. The people around me, wounded too, have to search their depths for answers. I can't help them. Shattered dreams lie at my husband's feet. I can't help him. All I can do is pray.

I was reading David Wilkerson's devotional and he said, "I can scarcely take it in when I read these words," "And the glory which Thou gavest me I have given them; that they may be one, even as we are one" (John 17:22). THIS IS GODS GLORY?? I'm seeing through the glass dimly, for sure.

This is where the "carnal mind" and the "spiritual mind" collide. I must decide in what realm I am going to exist – to doubt or to believe. Just believe that against all evidence in the natural, everything that screams, "Your life is over." Just believe God's got a plan, a glorious plan!! And it is going to unfold IF I WALK IN FAITH. "Look to the things above."

With every different season, I am reminded of what I used to do. I don't go looking for it. Out of the blue, it just smacks me in the face. The facts are irrefutable, if you're looking in the natural realm. I WANT, I NEED, TO GET OUT THAT REALM!!!

Surrender, surrender, surrender…Surrender everything, the horse, the guitar, the singing, the running, playing soccer, kickboxing, walking normally,

hiking with my husband, playing catch with Myles, walking in bare feet, ...
surrender. Look through Jesus's eyes. Look at what's really important.
Surrender the "things" and just believe. To be SPIRITUALLY MINDED
IS LIFE AND PEACE.

    Surrender was coming in stages. I was not there yet.

30. My Foot Raised from the Dead

It was wintertime 2011 the next time pain came knocking at my door, pain in my right foot, centering on my toes. As the day wore on, the pain increased and my foot began to darken, my big toe especially.

By this time we had engaged, considering my history, the VERY brave Dr. B. as my family physician. He's a family friend and, thankfully, a real "outside the box" thinking doctor. Dr B. was very similar to Doctor A., but even more unconventional. He advocated dietary change as a regular protocol is his practice. His office was new and located in our town, and it was booming. Young and old were coming to him, many with chronic health issues that had them dependent on a myriad of medications. People, when they took his advice, were getting well and free of drugs. The most dramatic of these was Robin, a woman about my age. She was on as many as 30+ medications a day. When we met, she was down to four medications and hoped to be weaned off those soon. Robin was back to work and going to school to renew her certification as a nursing assistant. All thanks to Dr. B. He works on the whole person: diet, lifestyle, coupled with some supplementation. People were getting their health back and word was getting out.

When I called Dr. B. to discuss what was happening with my foot, he thought at first it was a clot affecting the flow of blood. He suggested a few things and told us to call him in an hour if there was no change. The problem appeared to be resolved, but it began to hurt again, this time turning very dusky in color. Dr. B. said he'd come over to our house (who does that, these days?) and take a look at it. In less than half an hour, he was at the house, and after a few minutes of deliberation, he said we needed to go the ER at another hospital in the city. By the time Michael was pulling up to the door of the hospital, the foot was very dark in color and increasing in pain. Michael went to get me a wheelchair because walking on it was impossible. I was taken in to the treatment area in the back and given a room immediately. Several doctors came and consulted on what was happening to my foot. The mood of all the doctors was grim. I was admitted to the hospital. Tests were run and blood work was done. It was decided, after much deliberation, that it was a clot, although they did not find one on the scans. They told me that if the medication they gave me didn't work, I should understand that REMOVING MY FOOT would be the likely outcome of this event. Here we go again. Body parts, always more body parts. Having suffered through the past four years, I learned that God was going to see me through this no matter what happened. Even more than this, was my getting to KNOW the Lord in troubled times and I had seen Him bring "beauty out of the ashes." I was processing this as I lay there trying to cope with the pain, mulling over how I could ever surrender to such a fate, or, would I even have to.

The nursing staff was as kind as they could be, helping in any way they could. I felt safe and each one who came to my room seemed touched by my situation. Early in the morning on the second day, I was lying in my bed looking at my blackened foot. I had prayed the night before with Michael, but with no visible results. I was coming to grips with what the doctors had told me, *surrendering* to the fact that my foot would probably have to come off. As I lay there at six in the morning, studying my foot, it suddenly began to change in appearance. It was changing color. Very slowly it began to lose the dark black hue. The pain was lessening, and by the time two or three hours had gone by, some areas showed shades of pink. By the end of the day, most of my foot was back to normal with just a few patches of discolored skin. Come to find out one of the nurses I had the day before not only knew God, but believed He was still in the healing business. Dan Beardsley had been my daytime nurse and was touched by my plight. So that very morning at 6 AM, as he went for his morning walk, Dan began to pray for me and my dead, black foot. This is what he told me he said to the Lord. "God, you raised Lazarus from the dead. You can raise Barb's foot from the dead." Nothing fancy, just reminding God of His history. A heartfelt prayer borne on the wings of a heart of a brother that cared for a sister in Lord. As Dan prayed, my foot was returning to normal! All I can say is, when you are in trouble, it's good to know someone with connections! The doctors were all, collectively, scratching their heads.

I went home two days later, and over the next few weeks, my foot returned to normal, except for one toe. That toe took almost 20 months because one spot that just refused to heal. AND of course, IT HURT! I was referred to two highly recommended, podiatrists to try and figure out why it remained unhealed for so long. Checking the blood flow they discovered it was fine. That was not the problem. They were the specialists and they were stumped. During that time I suffered through unbelievable pain. This little spot had the capability to reduce me to sobbing, at times for hours. I could not wear a shoe that touched the toe. So for two years, I wore a sneaker that had the toe portion, cut out. At many times during this trial I felt I wanted have someone to just the darn toe off! "Just go ahead and lop it off"!! Dr. B. had given me pain medication and when I just could not take it anymore, I would use it, especially at night.

After many months, Dr. B. had a new natural product that he was vetting, and at one visit to his office, he asked me to try it. He told me that it accelerated the body's ability to heal; it is something that's native to our bodies. By this time, I had tried everything known to man to get this spot to heal, so I thought. I declined but decided to go home and do some research anyway. What I found out about supplementing with Redox Signaling Molecules sounded too good to be true. If it was true, then I was sure it would work. So I decided to take the plunge with yet another supplement. After one week of taking this "pool water," (that's what it tastes like), I was out of pain. One month later, it was healed over and the skin was beginning to look almost normal again. I was so thrilled to be able throw out my worn-out, "modified" sneaker. This also healed the colitis that was plaguing me off and on for six+ years since taking the Cipro. At times, I had been trapped at home for months.

Why would God heal the foot but leave this area unchanged? Why did this *miraculous* healing of my foot in the hospital, leave one spot yet unhealed? Beats me. All I can say is that, God's ways are not my ways. When I got on other side of it, I was changed again. I was very different. I was able to say, I KNOW my God.

The Holy Keep
Tuesday, April 13, 2010
The storehouse of the Lord. – where is it located? It's in our hearts waiting to be tapped into. "That Christ may dwell in our hearts by FAITH" Ephesians 3:17 "That you being ROOTED and grounded in love, may be able to comprehend...the depth, width, height, length...." of the fullness of God, His storehouse...the "Holy Keep."

In Malachi the Lord says, that in order to see the blessing the people had to turn their hearts BACK to HIM. He uses tithing as an analogy. He told them to bring into the storehouse what they should have been giving all along. The tithe is the HEART! He wanted their hearts!!" NOT THEIR CASH! He wants every corner of our heart, even the dark corners, because once He's inside the corners are full of light!! "Return to Me and I will return unto you".

Malachi 3:10 says "Prove Me now herewith.... if I will not open to you the windows of heaven, and POUR you out a blessing that there shall not be room enough to receive it."

Ephesians 3:19,20 "Now to Him that is able to do exceedingly ABUN-DANTLY ABOVE all that we ask or think." The blessing of the Lord His storehouse, His fullness, is accessed by grace, by obedience, by turning to Him with your whole heart. All these things are fueled by FAITH.

Wikipedia describes the keep "A keep is a strong central tower which is used as a fortress. Often the keep is the most defended area of a castle, and as such may form the main habitation area, or contain important stores such as the armory, food, and the main water well, which would ensure survival during a siege." That's faith, our strong tower!

It "passes knowledge." Ephesians 3:19 – "He is able to do exceedingly, abundantly, above all that we ask or think!!"

Jeremiah 17:8 – The man whose trust/faith is in the Lord, he is "like a tree planted by the waters, and spreads out her roots by the river and shall not suffer when the heat comes, but her leaf shall be green and not suffer in the year of drought nor cease from yielding fruit." When you are plugged into the Lord BY FAITH, your access to the storehouse, the Holy Keep, is unlimited.

Faith, Faith, Faith!!! Fear and doubt,limit your access to God's Holy Keep.

31. The New Portrait You Paint

Every stroke has a different signature on the body, as different as snowflakes. Sometimes their imprint is subtle. More often than not, their effects are life altering. When the dust settles, the bits and pieces to be picked up again, can create a very different portrait of the person you were pre-stroke. This is as cruel as MS or Parkinson's. Anything that now dictates what you can or cannot do is going to affect you like no other thing could. The human race is geared towards *doing*, and what you DO oftentimes DEFINES who you are. It did me, without my realizing it. The more you *did* prior to the stroke, the greater the adjustment.

You never want to let others set your boundaries or limits how far you can go. A stroke is not as easy to resist. Push the envelope EVERY DAY! Some of my doctors felt we should not be surprised if I could not walk again. To this I said, "Peanut butter, Peanut butter." Those survivors who beat the odds and progressed further than predicted by health care experts, have worked their tails off. Doctors can't know every thing about what is going to heal in your brain and what isn't. Attitude in one's approach to recovery is key. I had a "can do," or "fighter" personality to begin with and I thank God that trait survived the stroke. I know of a woman who had a stroke just about the time I had mine. Barb Kelly is now just beginning to walk. Six + years after her stroke, she is defying the odds and learning to walk again. I know another woman who had a stroke while in labor with her first child. The stroke and recovery time robbed her of her being able to bond with her son. So, Renee Sorensen, despite her disabilities, went on to have another child. She raised that baby single-handed, literally. I have seen others where that drive is lost completely, leaving a spouse with a great sense of loss. Where did the person I married go? Stroke survivors, who get stuck in the depression, and never get past the anger stage of what has happened to them, are robbed of their potential.

I feel I have squeezed out of my body everything it has to give, and I'm not finished. I had at my disposal some very loving and talented practitioners. This was so important. If I was to pick two elements, or "tools" that I believe are premier in helping stroke survivors recover, they would be hyperbaric chamber and redox signaling molecules in supplement form (ASEA)*. I would do them ASAP. I say this knowing what I know now, having experienced the healing power of both. Then, I would do cranial sacral therapy, Chiropractic and Tailwind. The first year is so critical for recovery. There is healing that can happen later, but you have to really squeeze it out of those modalities after the first year.

It is hard for others to NOT define you by your stroke. The least favorite greeting that I still get six+ years out is, with the inquirer's head tilted and a pouting mouth, "How are you feeling?" I don't know if it's the head tilt, the pout, or the question that bothers me most, but I know in their eyes, I AM broken and they will always relate to me as being broken. I'm always tempted to give a smart aleck reply such as, "With my hands, like everyone else." So far, I've restrained myself. It was December 18, 2007 when my stroke occurred, and believe or not, I still get asked that question. Despite keeping my household running, cooking meals everyday, driving any and everywhere, milking goats, making soap and cheese, selling at the Farmers Market, gardening, etc. I haven't even had a COLD in almost three years!! Come on, people, let me move onward.

Most of the time I don't see myself in the light of my stroke. Those little areas only pop up their heads when something that I used to do confronts me and the task shows itself to be impossible. Usually that is because of being one-handed. Occasionally, when I am struggling with a tasks and a family member tries to insert themselves to help me, my first response is to just growl. I can never get the words out fast enough to say, "That's okay. Let me try a little longer, dear." Growling seems to just come out without my thinking about it. I'm learning to avoid those tasks, or situations, and just plow full steam ahead in the things I can do, with one hand tied behind my back, just

to make it fair, To compromising with grace, not despising my limitations but recognizing that God can use me in ways He never would have before. I'm back to milking goats, one handed, (it's not pretty) making cheese, (very messy) and soap, (occasionally dangerous). I started a business with the goat milk soaps and I make and sell several tinctures and salves, at local stores.

Having looked over the edge, "looked the proverbial elephant 'dead in the eye'," and have proven to myself that every life has worth. Who knows where the ripples end from this life-changing event?

"In this you greatly rejoice, though now, for a little while, if need be, you have been grieved by various trials, that the genuineness of your faith, being much more precious than gold that perishes, though it is tested by fire, maybe found to praise honor, and glory at the revelation of Jesus Christ." – 1 Peter 1:6-7. As I write this, I can tell you I could not comprehend the "rejoicing" part of that scripture, never mind "greatly rejoicing," in the heat of my trial. Now, on the other side, I grasp the value of a genuine faith. It is truly a *high tower* and a *rock* to stand on.

Why did I decide to include how my faith helped me through this time? My goal was to tell the whole story, to relate every detail, including the huge part that my faith played in my recovery. God who is, I believe, the author of human life, is the most qualified in healing the wounds of this traumatic event, spirit, soul, emotions, and body. It is because of my faith in Him, beauty has risen out of this heap of ashes. Stripped away was every-thing but my family, every-thing I held dear, all that made up "me" as a whole, functioning person. It was like starting all over again, from a form of infancy. My development returning from this place of destruction was a brief span in time compared to true infancy. Still, it included many challenges, heartbreaks, victories, emotion, dangers, and fears, not unlike my growing up.

There was a period when I was concerned about stroking again. Reoccurring stroke can be rather common if steps are not taken to prevent such an event. In the winter, my blood thickens a lot. So I take a preventative regimen of supplements. I increase my Omega 3, Krill oil. I take Nattokinaise, Astaxanthin and Enzymes. These are the major players in my supplements. Then I take others that support all-around good health, plus my diet is very strict, healthy!! I don't do sugar, anymore, not even brownies. Try not to buy GMO foods and I garden in the summer, eating organic, when I can.

Here I am six years out from this season of devastation; I am a different person in a lot of ways. My ability to articulate is diminished, I get frustrated in a debate, especially if it's on the phone. I've been known to hang up in pure frustration, go have a good cry, gather myself and call back in 15 minutes. My personality, the old me, usually shows up when I'm at the keyboard typing. It feels like to me, a more level playing field, even if it's only in my head.

I don't enjoy going into a room filled with strangers, all with "tilted heads" and "pouting" expression looking at me. It is near impossible to make an entrance under the radar when you're walking like a drunk, and using a cane. I remind people of their own mortality. So most don't think to themselves, "Hmmm. I'd like to talk to her." No, rather, as though strokes were contagious, they steer clear, giving wide berth to one so afflicted by life.

I find those who do engage me are very comfortable in their own skin. Who they are in no way is related to the state I find myself in. I am seeing this as a chance to study human nature.

At the grocery store recently, there was a gentleman asking people if they want try some, "Award-winning" wine. He engaged <u>everyone</u> that walked by, but me. Maybe he thought by the way I walked, I was already "sampling" the wine at home. I finished up shopping, but I had forgotten my debit card. So, I went out to my car to retrieve it. On way back through, I passed by him again. He avoided eye contact, and looked past me to engage someone walking behind me. I was tempted to thank him, because I decided that he must have thought I was not old enough. The legal drinking age is 21. THAT MUST by why!

"It is not about you." Before my stroke, it never was. I'm starting to regain this truth, as I put distance between myself and these events. It takes being others centered. "Forgetting what lies behind, press on to those things that are ahead."(Phil 3:13)

I've realized how much my state of mind controls my physical abilities. If I feel tense or unsure of myself, my legs just don't work. If I am relaxed and not thinking too much about anything, I can walk semi-normally, never smoothly, but better. I cannot walk and talk at the same time very well, Multitasking is very difficult. When I'm upset, my right arm raises up from my shoulder like I'm getting ready to fly or launch a one-armed attack. That is a sure warning sign to anyone arguing with me. When I am stressed the right side of my top lip goes in to the scowl position, just the right side. Nice. Really gives me a certain edge, or persona, during a debate. When I stand up from the prone position, my body REQUIRES that I stretch. God help me if we ever have a fire during the night. "Where is mom?" "I'm stretching, be right there." Again, even though these are the facts that pertain to my body now, they are not sifted through the filter of "Oh. I had a stroke."

I now have the attention span of a gnat, and am easily distracted by the oxygen in the air. In a conversation, someone will be speaking, I'll think of a response to meet the flow of conversation, and in a minute, the thought is gone. This can be very frustrating. On the phone sometimes, I will jot notes to myself that keep my thoughts or responses fresh in the fore front of my mind. This IS the new me. I have dealt with it. Now lets go on and see what's next!! It is never a dull moment with my "new" body.

I look around me and seen the ravages of stroke and its effects on others and I am so grateful, that I have been allowed to gain so much back. Gratitude is going to carry me all the days of my life.

I will close with wise words of Winston Churchill, who is a revered historical figure in our family. He speaks to the, spirit, the heart and soul of men, as few can. Two of his quotes spoke to me during my seven-year ordeal. The first was, "Never, never, never give in!" The second, which is very practical advice for us all: "If you are going through hell, keep going."

*http://drrobwebinar.com/ —-informative video
aseacellhealth1@gmail.com —-questions/comments

32. No Ones Talking

I asked my family to tell how the stroke affected them. It was like pulling teeth. None revisit that time willingly. Finally, Sam opened up. He was 14 at the time of my stroke:

Looking back to those months prior to the stroke, I remember mostly the in and out of the hospital and the lack of improvement. Being around 14 at the time, I was more of the mindset that, I had no part to play in anything that went on, but to pray, and do whatever I was told to do in order to help out. Just after the stroke happened, my little brother Myles, and I went to spend Christmas and New Year's with our Aunt Jo's and Uncle V.J.'s family. I wasn't totally sure the reason why. This put me entirely out of the picture of what was happening, or of the all the details. The first time seeing Mom after getting back from my stay with my aunt and uncle, I had no idea that a stroke had taken place. I am usually the last to know things, whether due to the fact that I can be absorbed in something completely or that being number 5 out 6 boys puts me in a position to be lost in the crowd. I assumed wrongly, (as I often do,) that Mom's state of not be able to move or talk was due to the medication. Well, in a roundabout ways, I suppose this is true, it was the medication that brought on the stroke.

Today, when I talk to friends of the family there is not much to report that is new. Still unable to use her right arm and her right leg is limited in it use. There is nothing exciting to report BUT that does not mean there is nothing remarkable to report. Even with these challenges Mom doesn't slow down. Months after the stroke, when she was able to use a wheelchair, she would act as the supervisor and point and give directions. As soon as she was able to stand she was doing dishes. When she was able to walk she started cooking meals again. To follow, was weeding her garden. Most scary was when she started driving (strangely through I still feel safer with her than driving with my Dad, sorry Dad.) Then it was milking our goats then using the milk to make soap, doing farmers markets. The list goes on. I was only allowed to help Mom when there was no way around it. So, no matter how much I wanted to help when Mom would struggle with something if she could do it, there was no way to be able to lend a hand. Now this is what I can tell friends of the family, not that "Mom has made a full recovery," but that "Mom has few limitations!"

As a closing note I'll leave you with one of Mom's and my first victories together. It was a few weeks after Mom came home from the hospital and she was stuck in bed. She was still unable to talk, but she could use her left arm. I checked to see if there was anything I could get. Thus began one of the LONGEST games of one-armed charades/20…120 questions I have ever been party to. Mom motioned with her thumb and index finger that she wanted something square. So I went down the list, Remote, radio, and so on. By the end we were in hysterics, me crying, Mom laughing. Finally I said "brownie" and that was the ticket. I was shocked. Mom was never one to eat a lot of sweets. Even though it took at least half an hour to get it, we saw it though. In closing, I just would like to say: Mom and Dad, thanks for being two of the greatest examples of perseverance anyone could ever have.

About five months after my stroke Myles, who was six at onset of this journey, had a very pointed observation.

Out of the Mouth of Babes
Thursday, April 17, 2008

Vanity dies a slow painful death, but today, I think it took a death blow. Myles was talking about how I've changed in the five months since the stroke. He talked about how much I can do now, walking, ever so slowly, and now I can lift my arm up, and I can talk some. He wrapped up the observations with how much my face has changed. "You aren't beautiful anymore, but I still love you.

"That's good" I said, "Because you are stuck with me."

Epilogue

In the process of writing, over the past three years, as God continued to heal my heart, it was made clear that this story is not about the hospital. It was never my goal to make the hospital "central" in my story. What I hope to convey to the reader is, that there is a burning torch, to light the way in any trial. That, at every turn in my journey, there was mercy and grace extended to me. My enemy was on a leash. When the storms in this life are raging, there is hope. That light is God, the creator of the universe. Who, by His breath, breathed the stars into existence. (Psalm 33:6) The Maker of heaven earth, extends a loving hand with promise to carry us through anything we face. John 3:16 says: "For God so loved the world that He sent His only begotten Son, that whoever believes in Him should not perish but have everlasting life." Now, THAT is an awesome deal!!